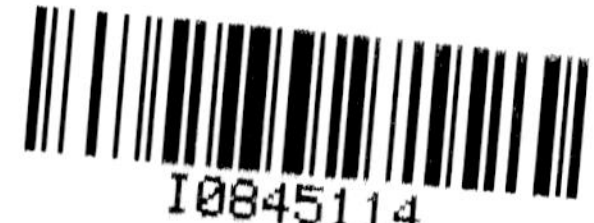
I0845114

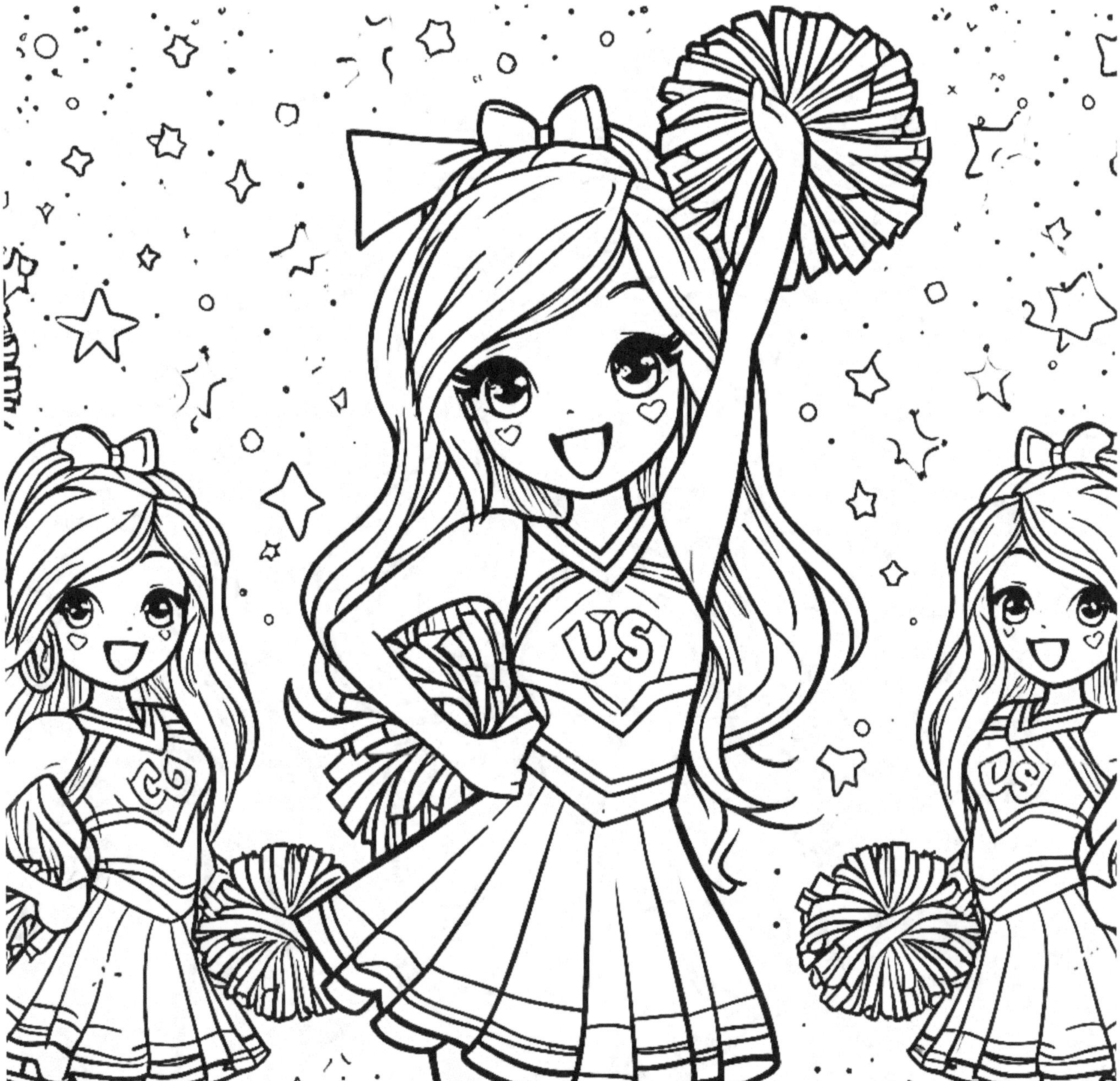

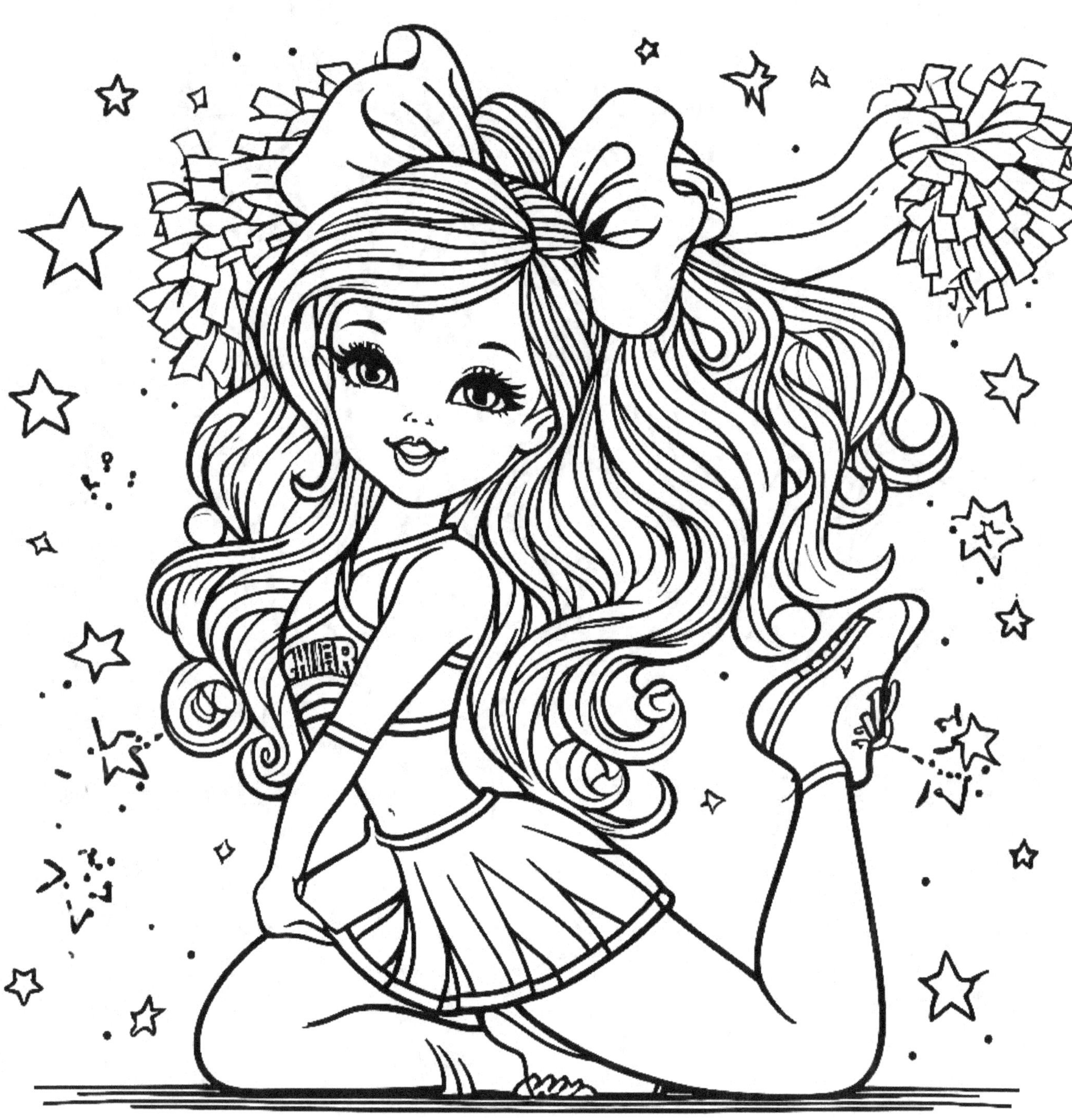
CHEER

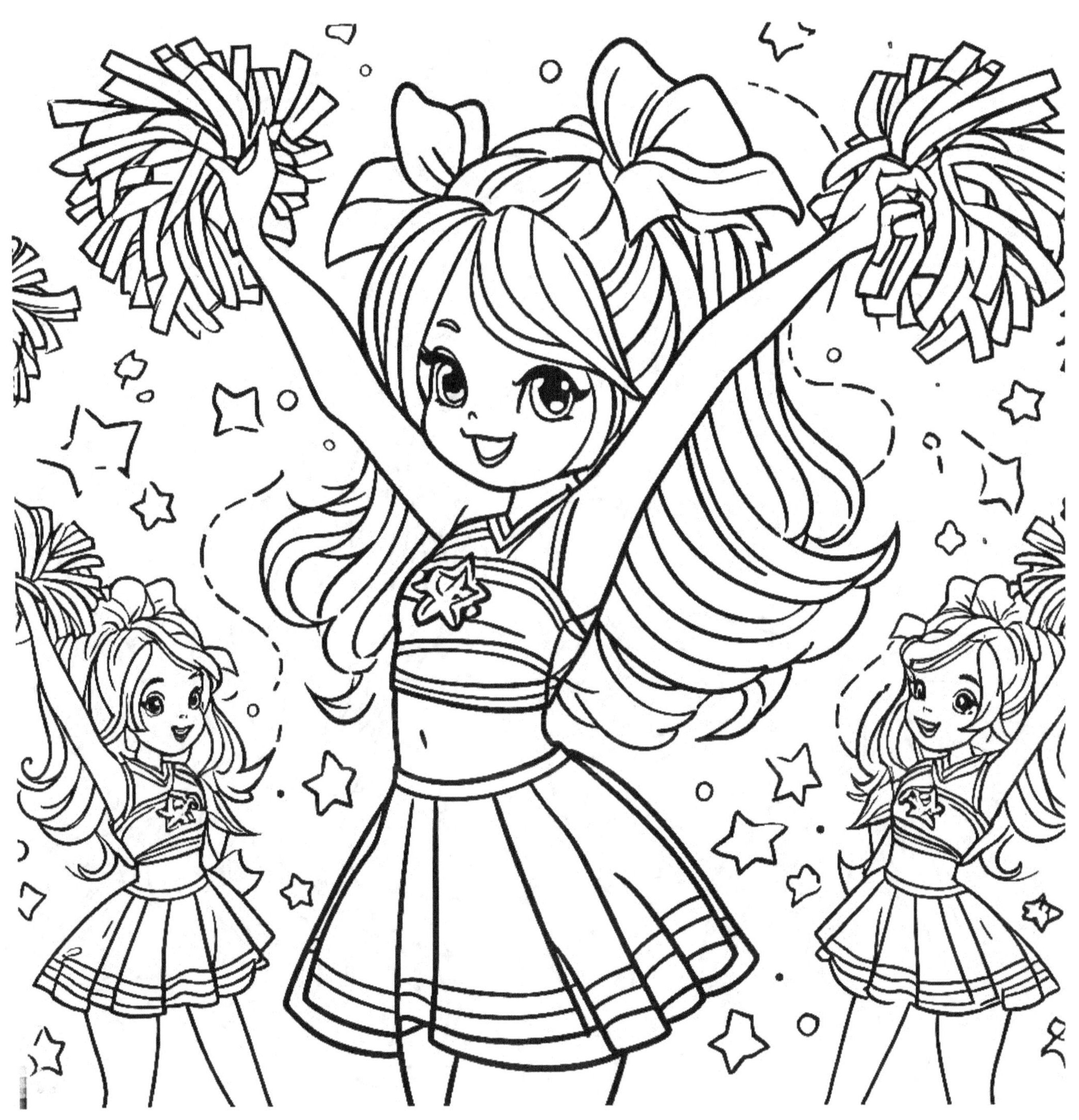

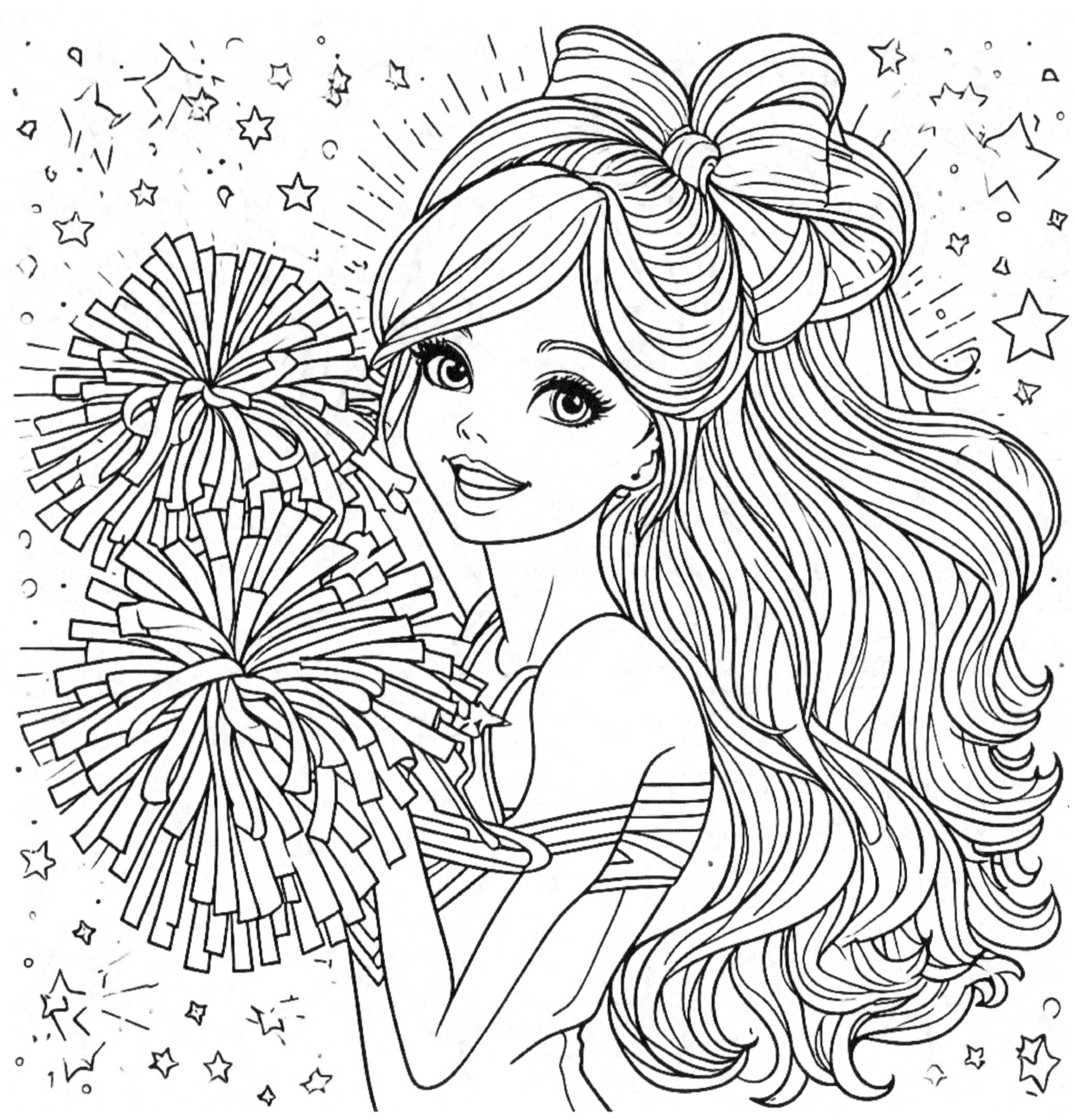

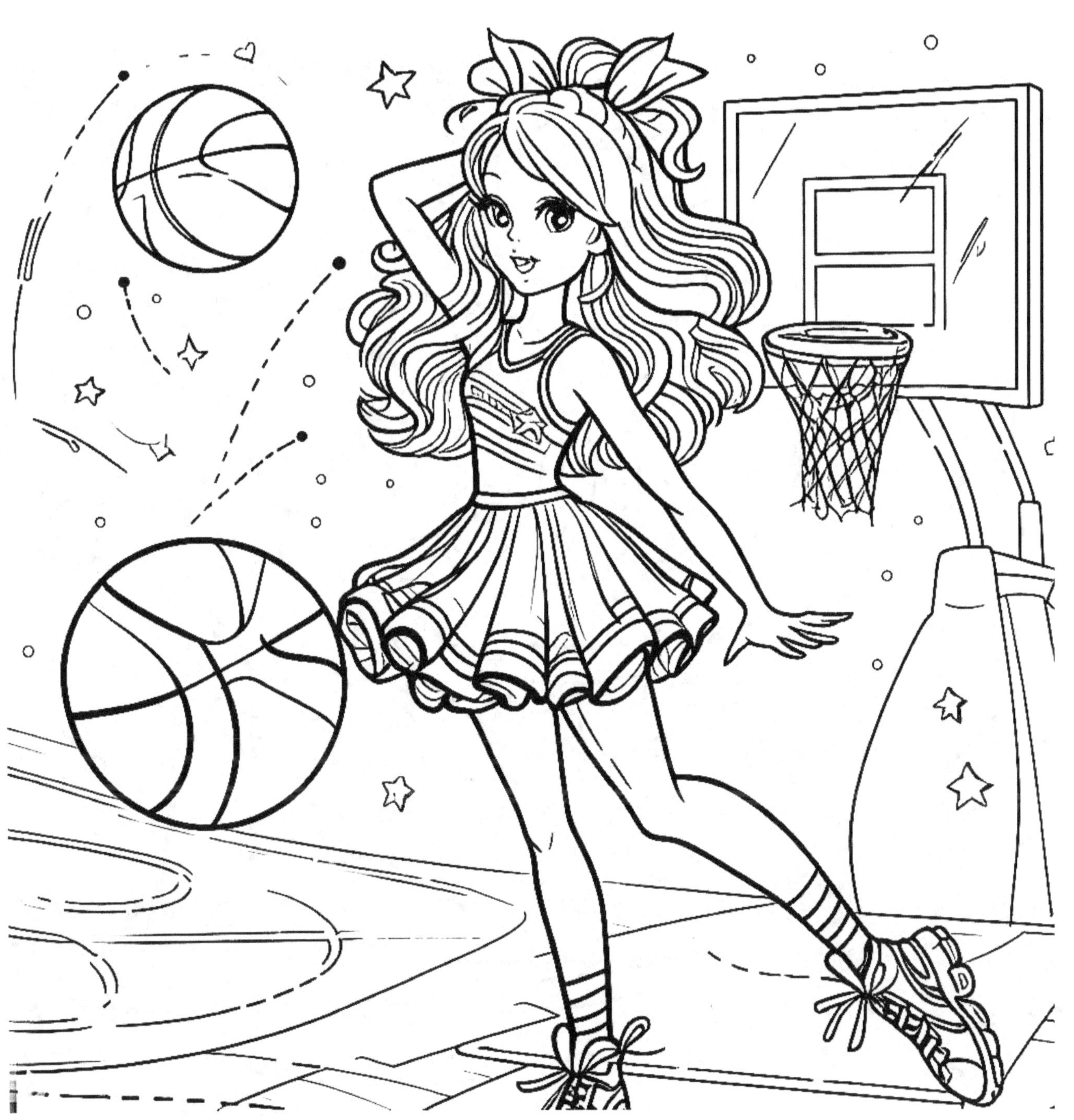

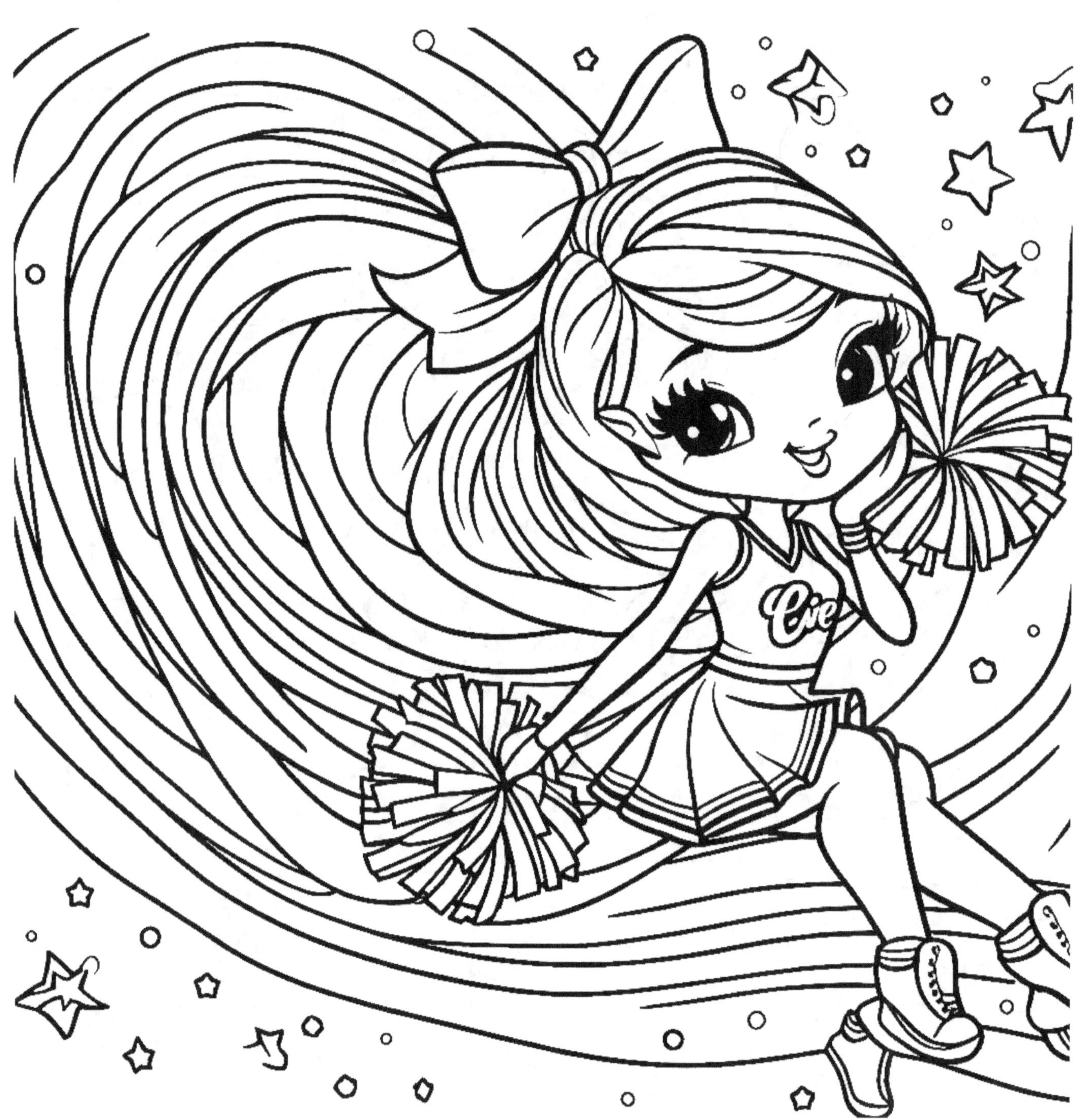

Evie

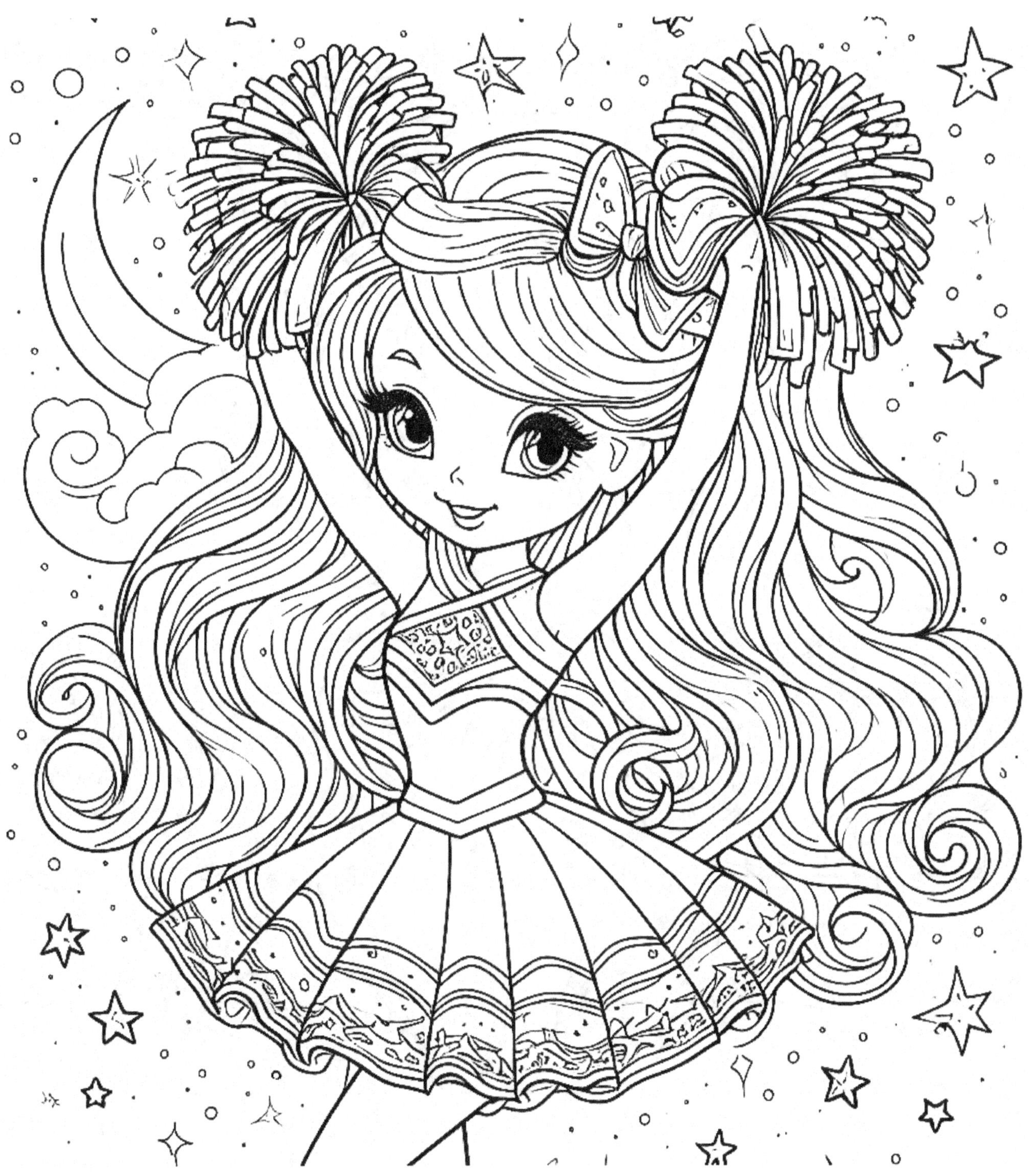

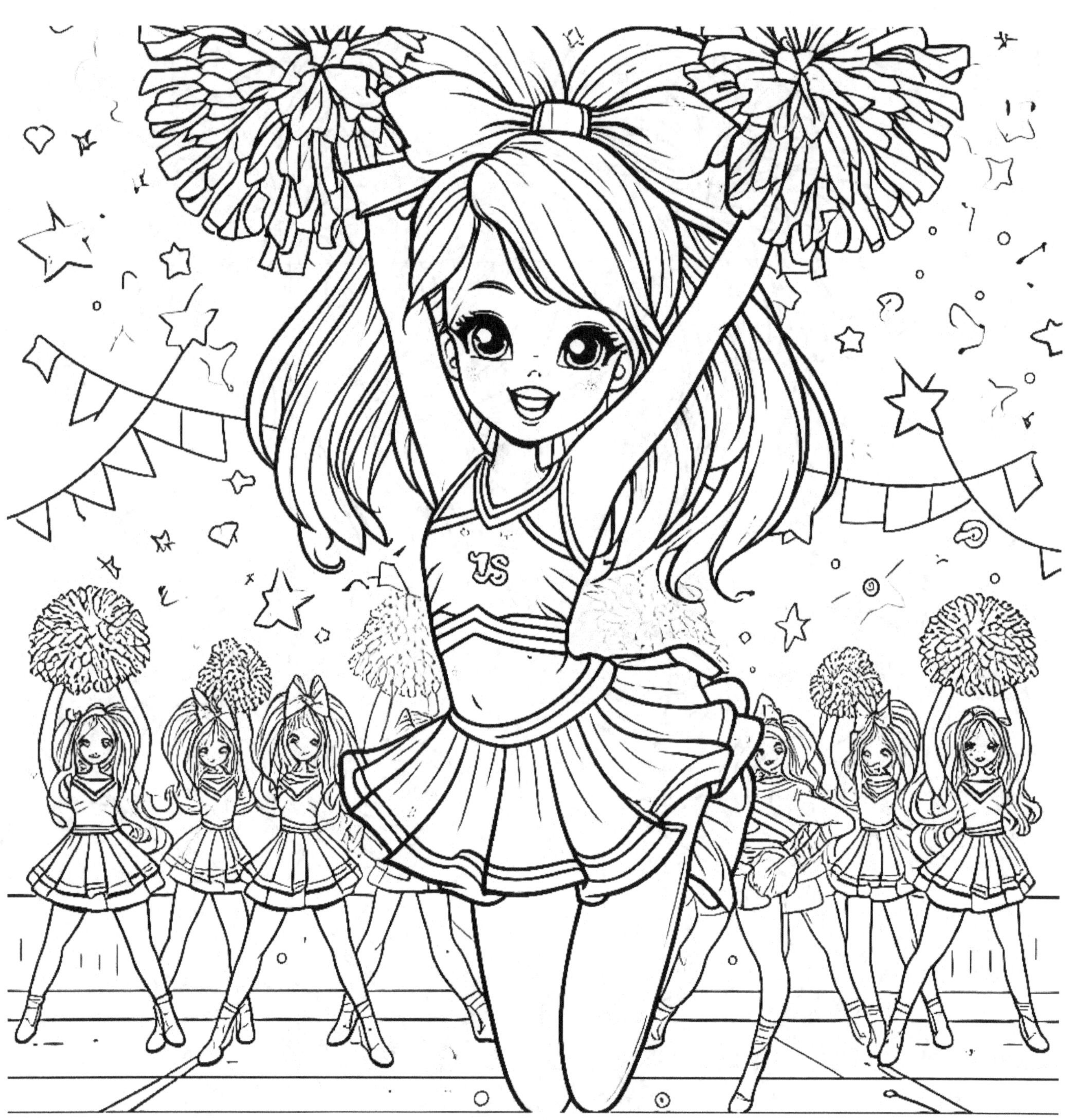

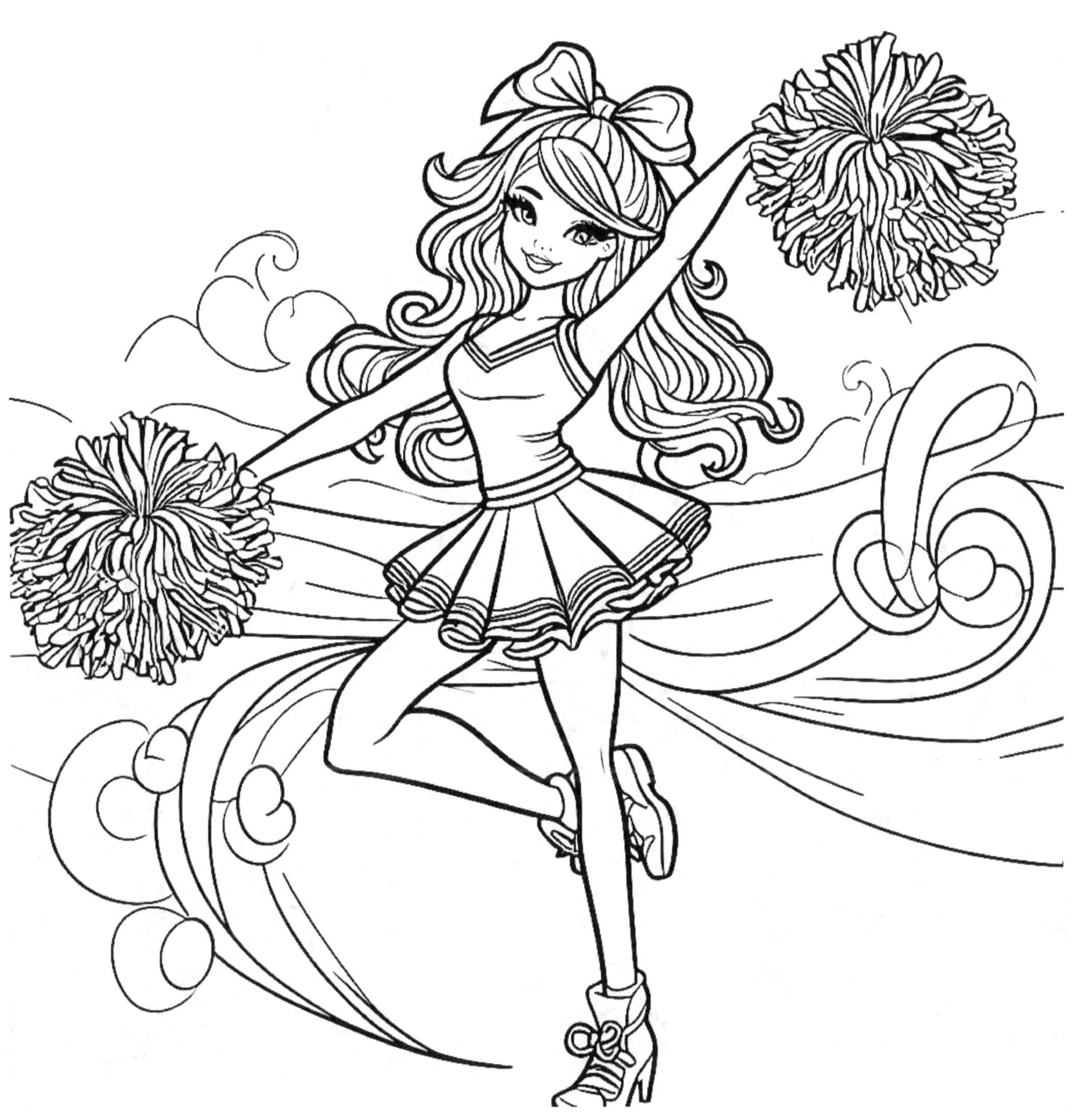

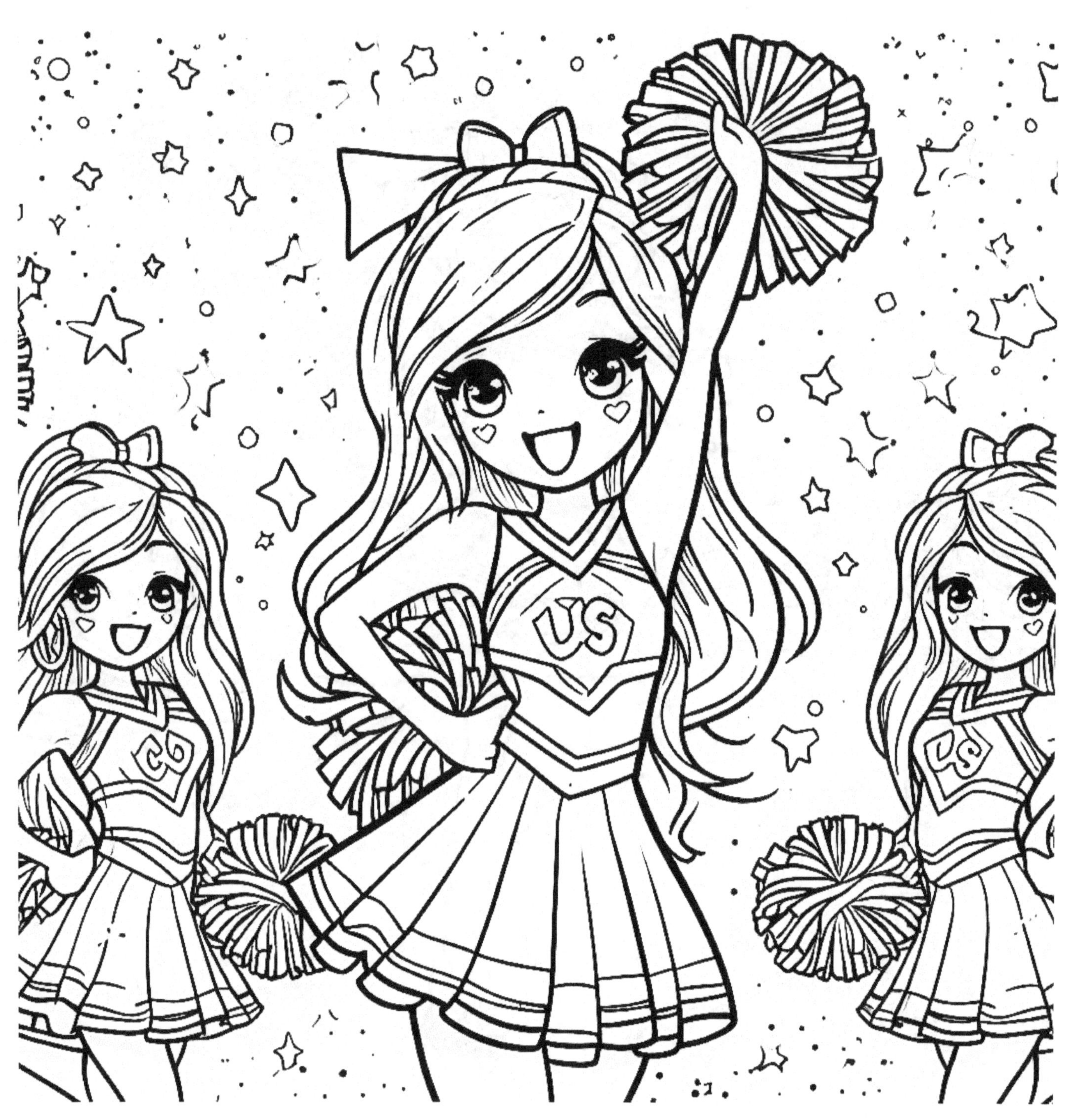

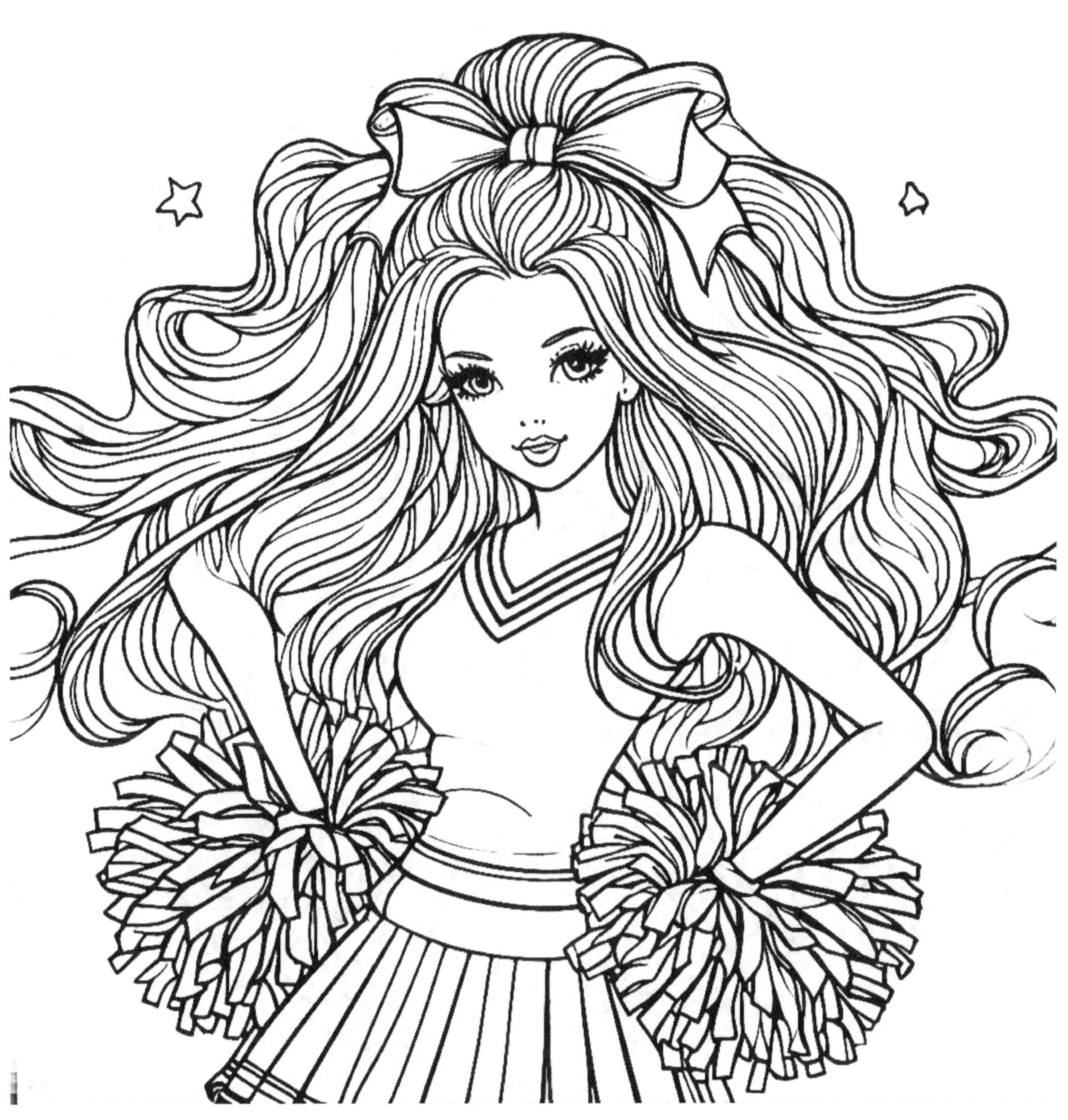

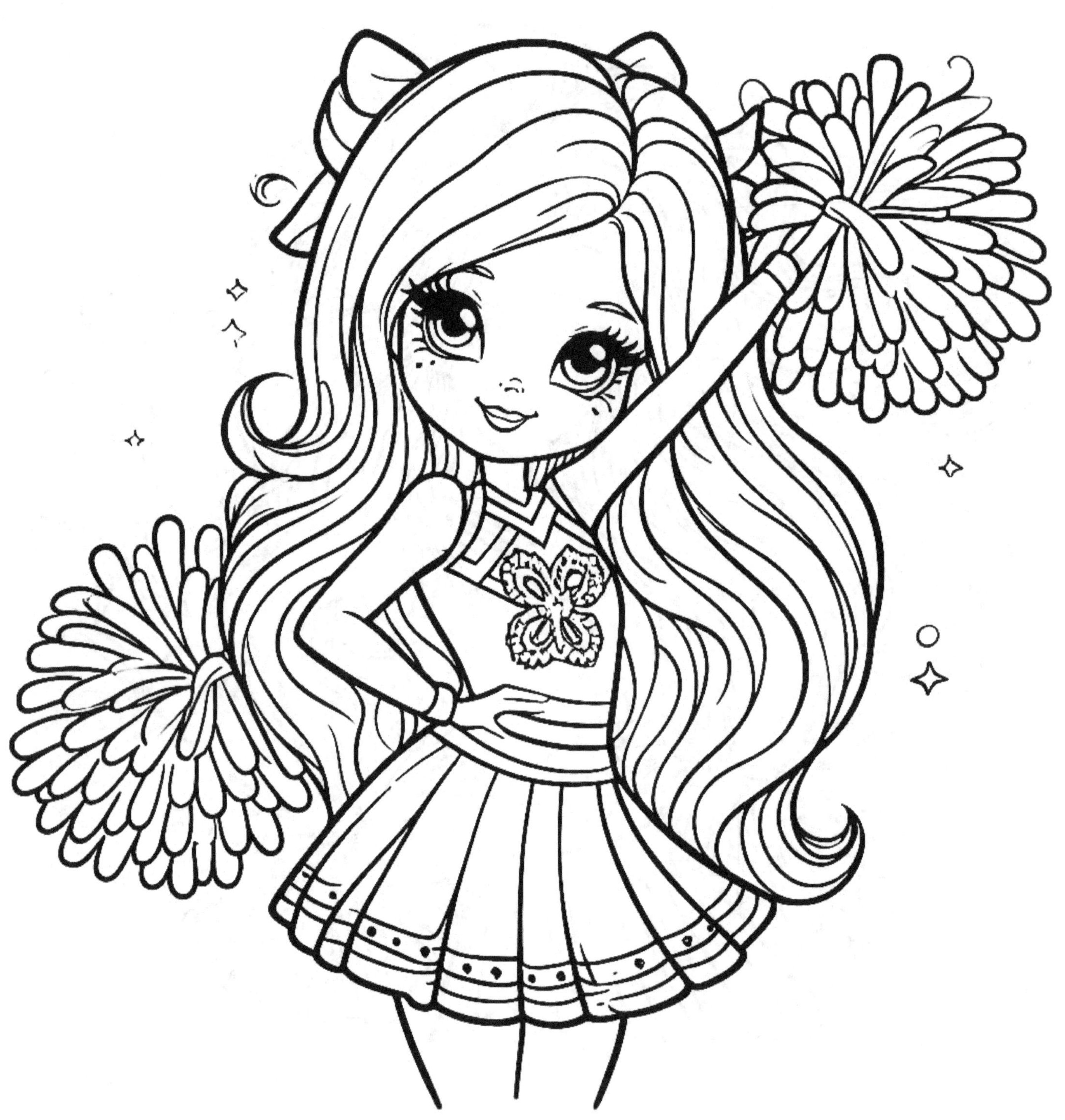

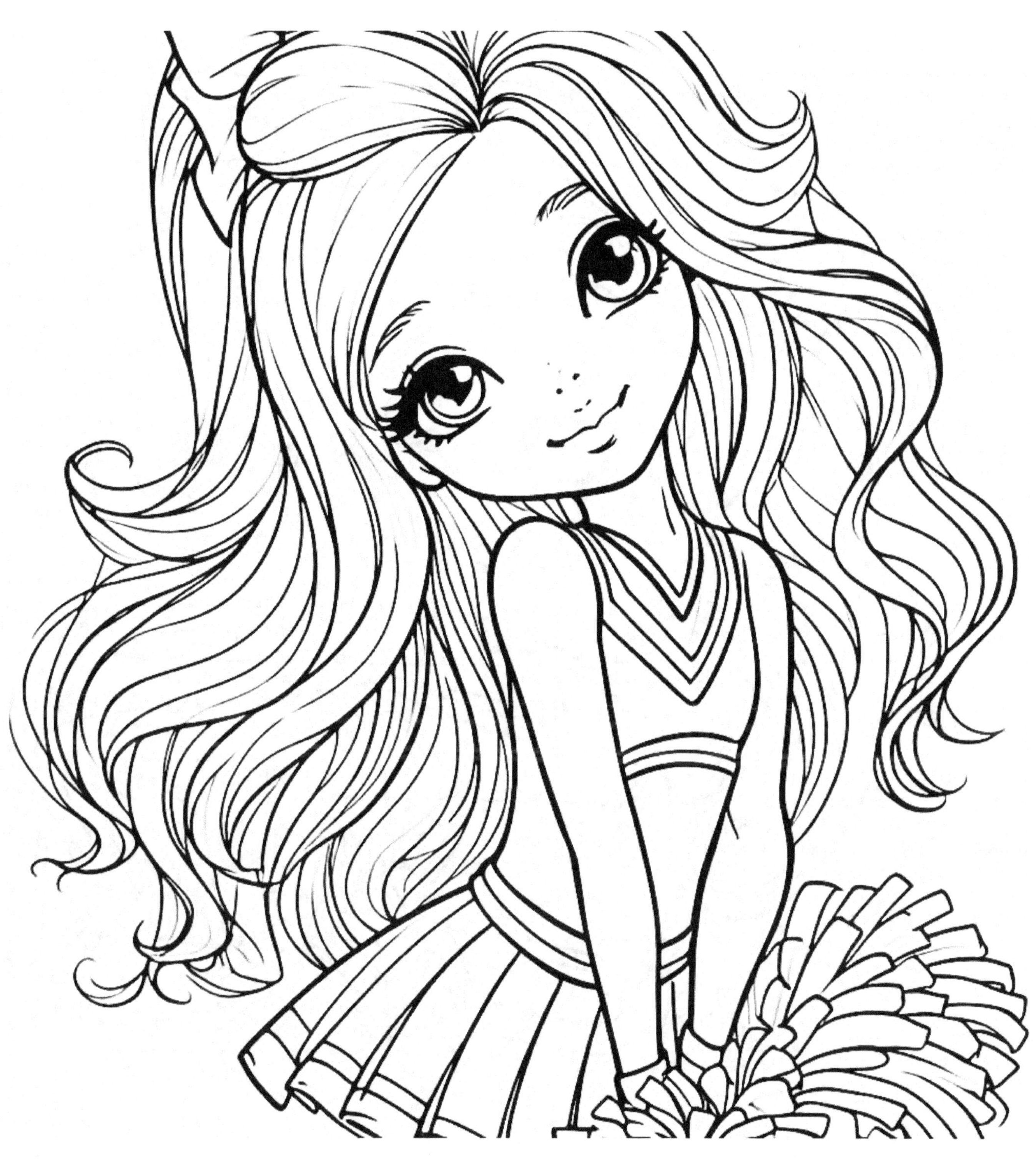

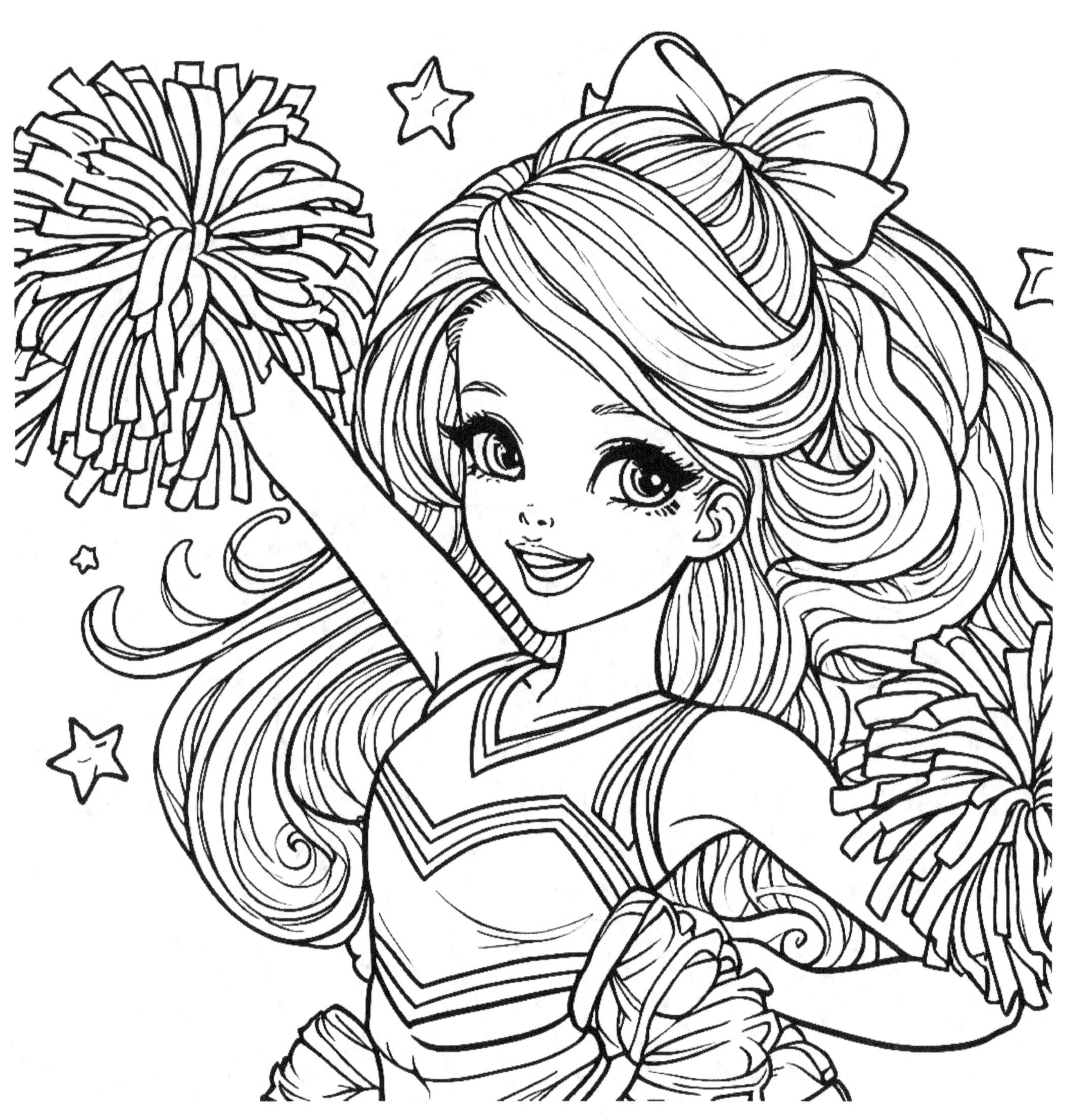

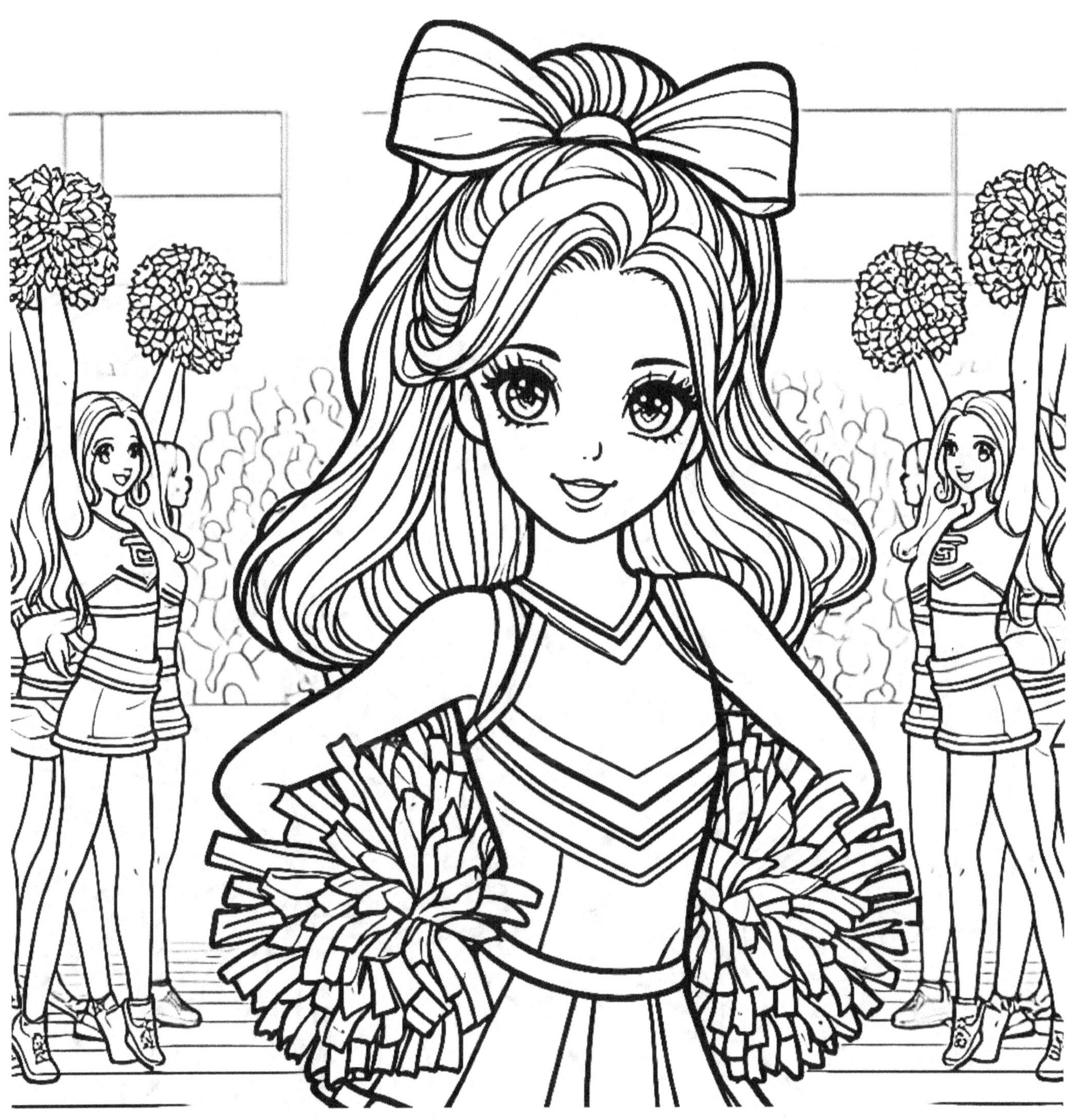

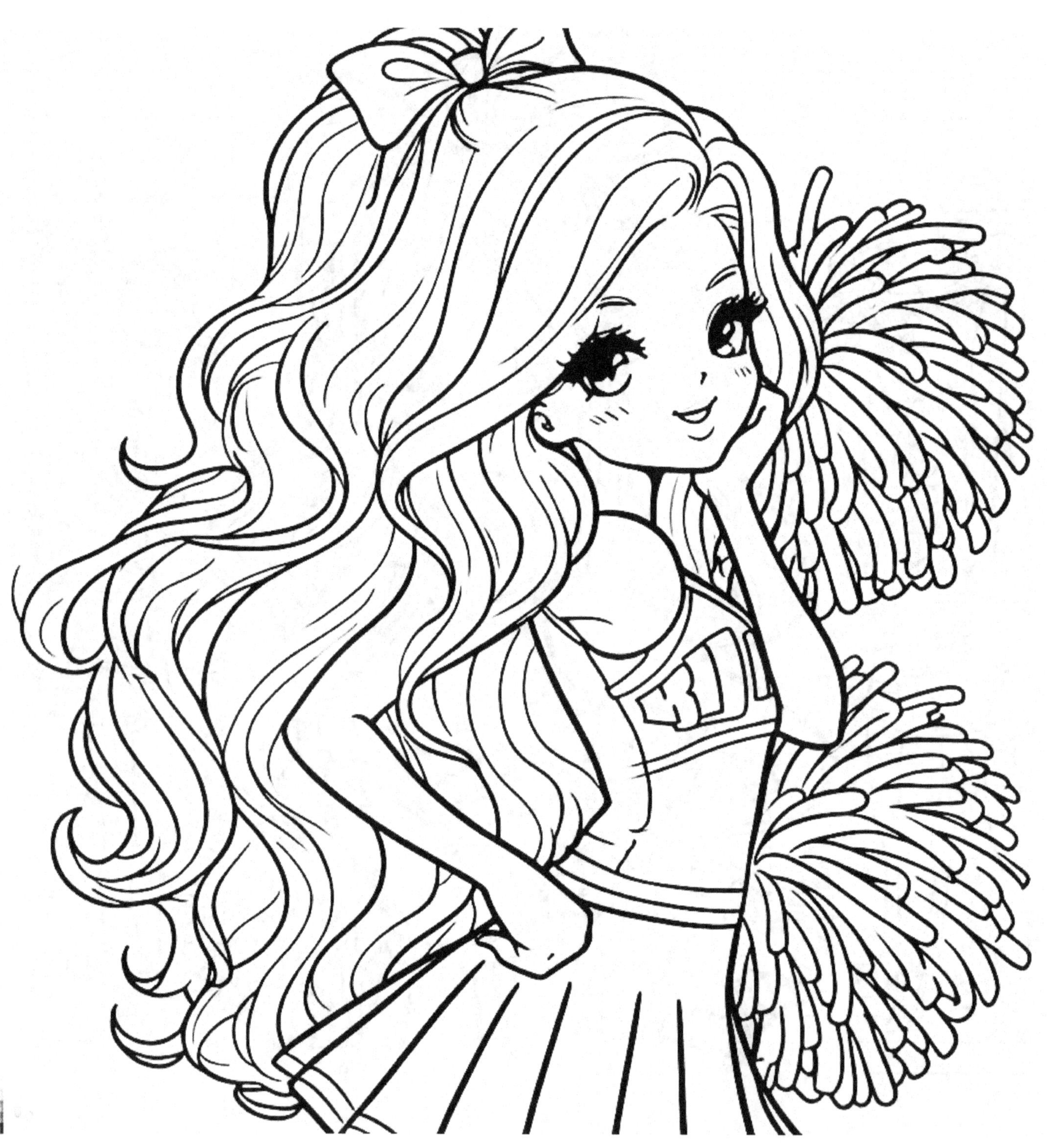

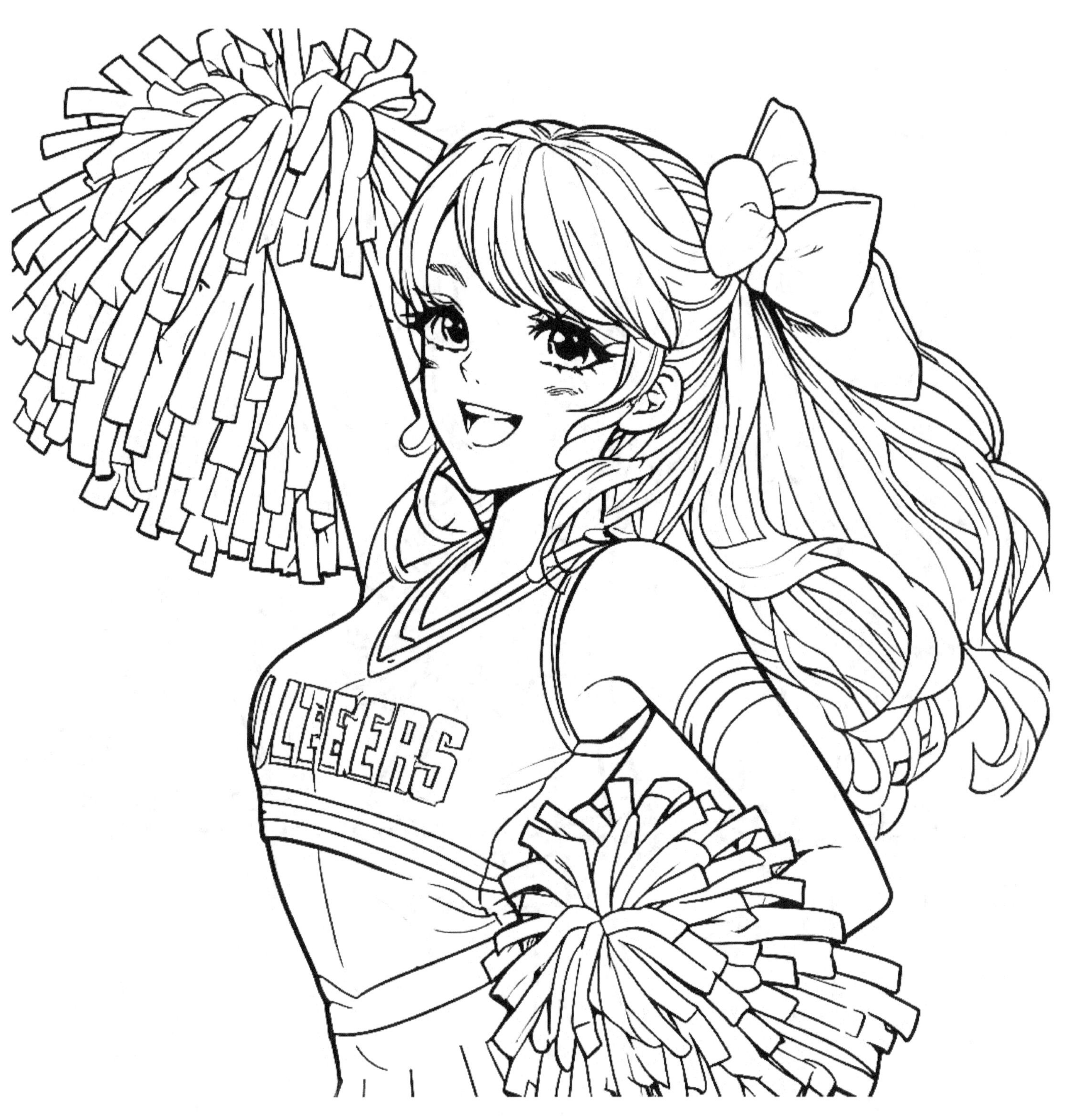
OLLEERS

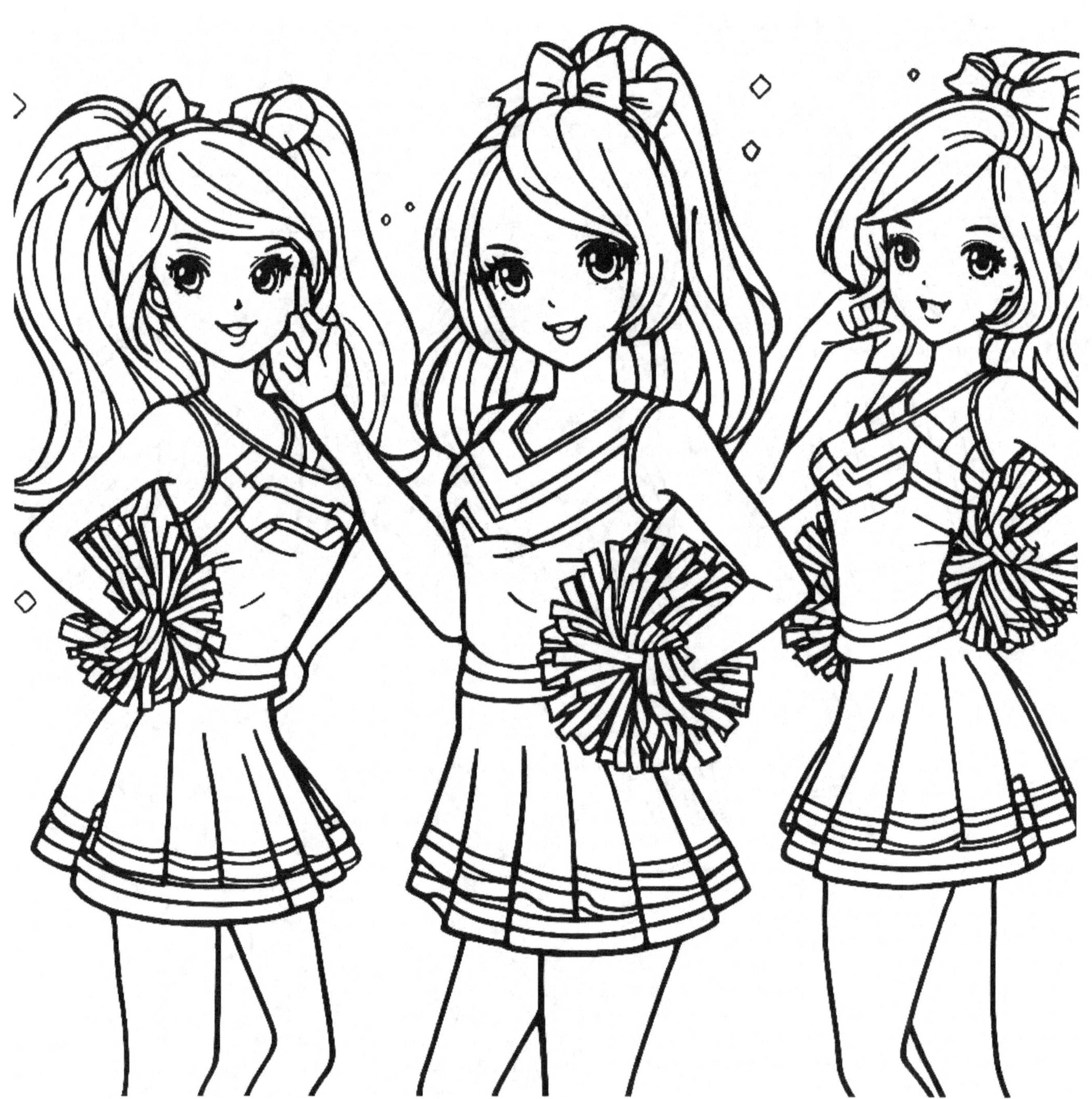

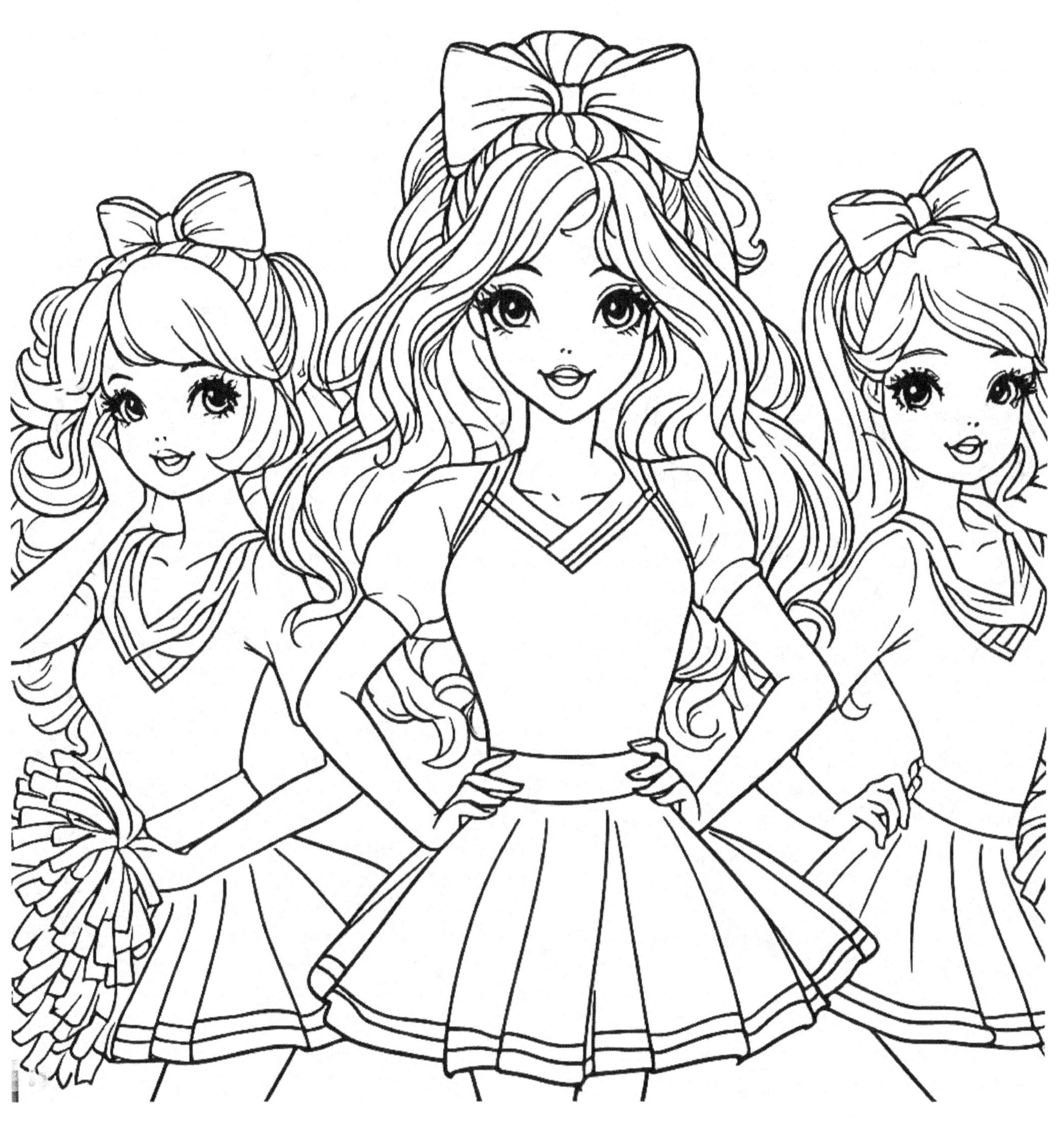

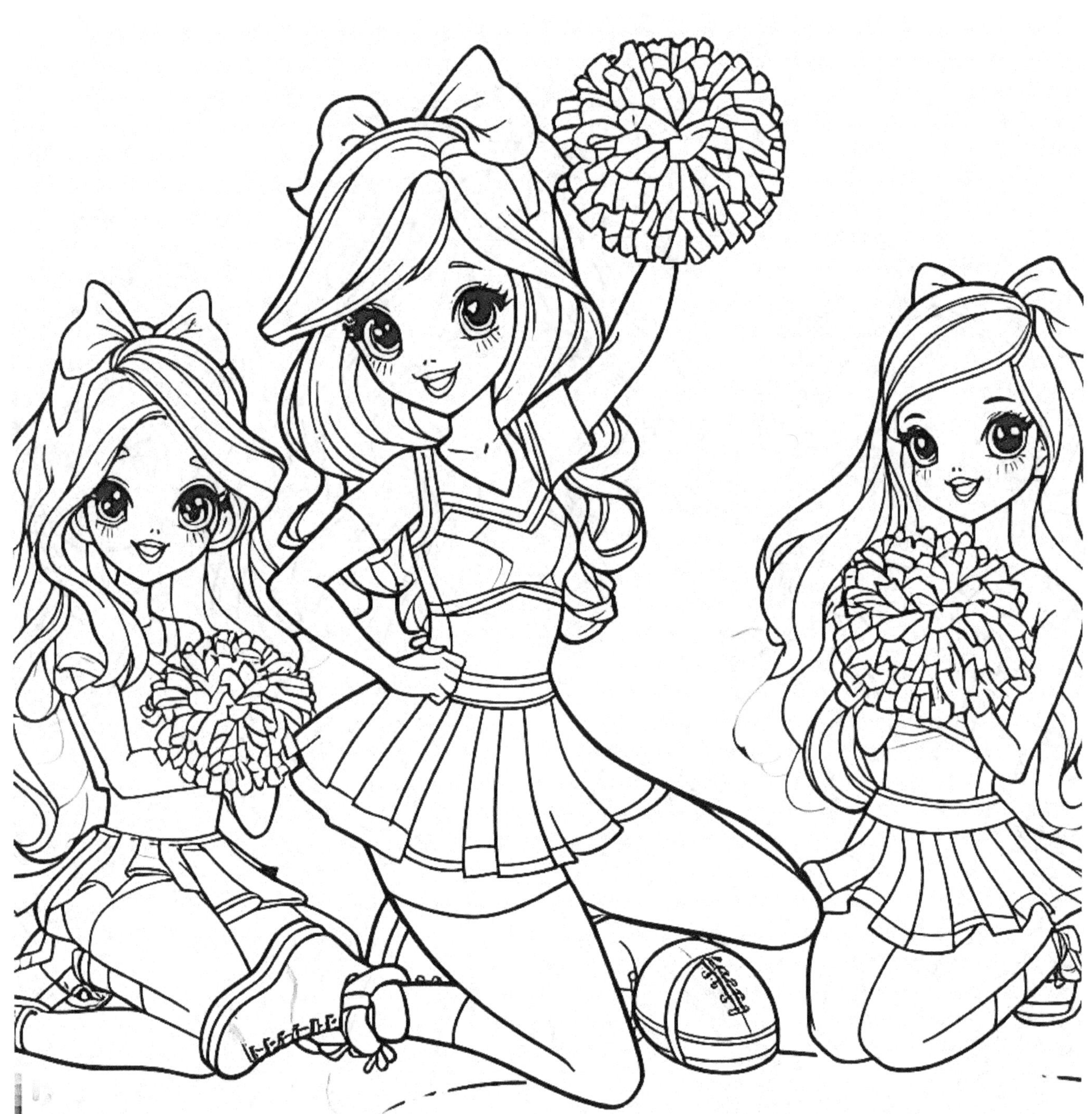

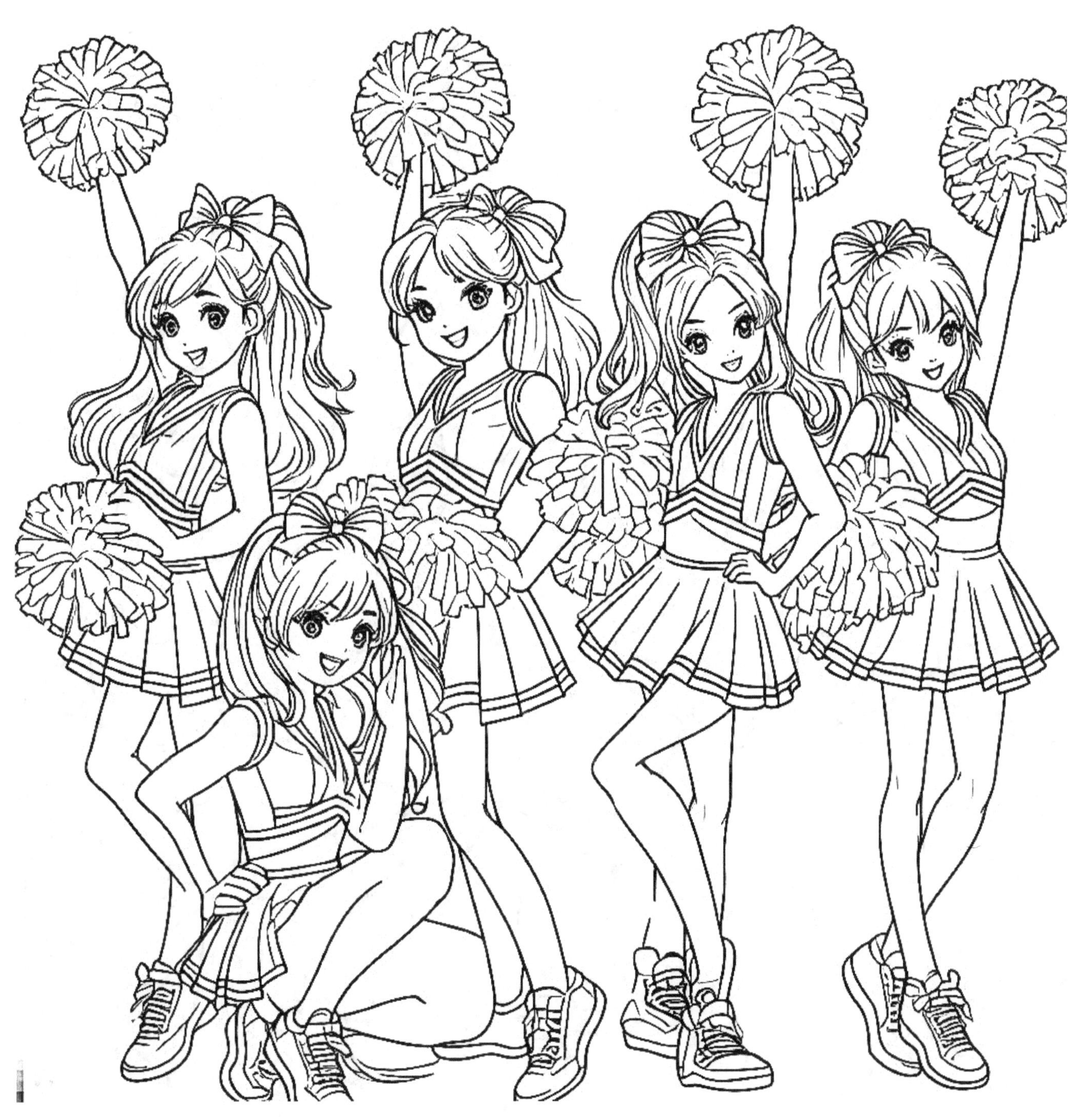

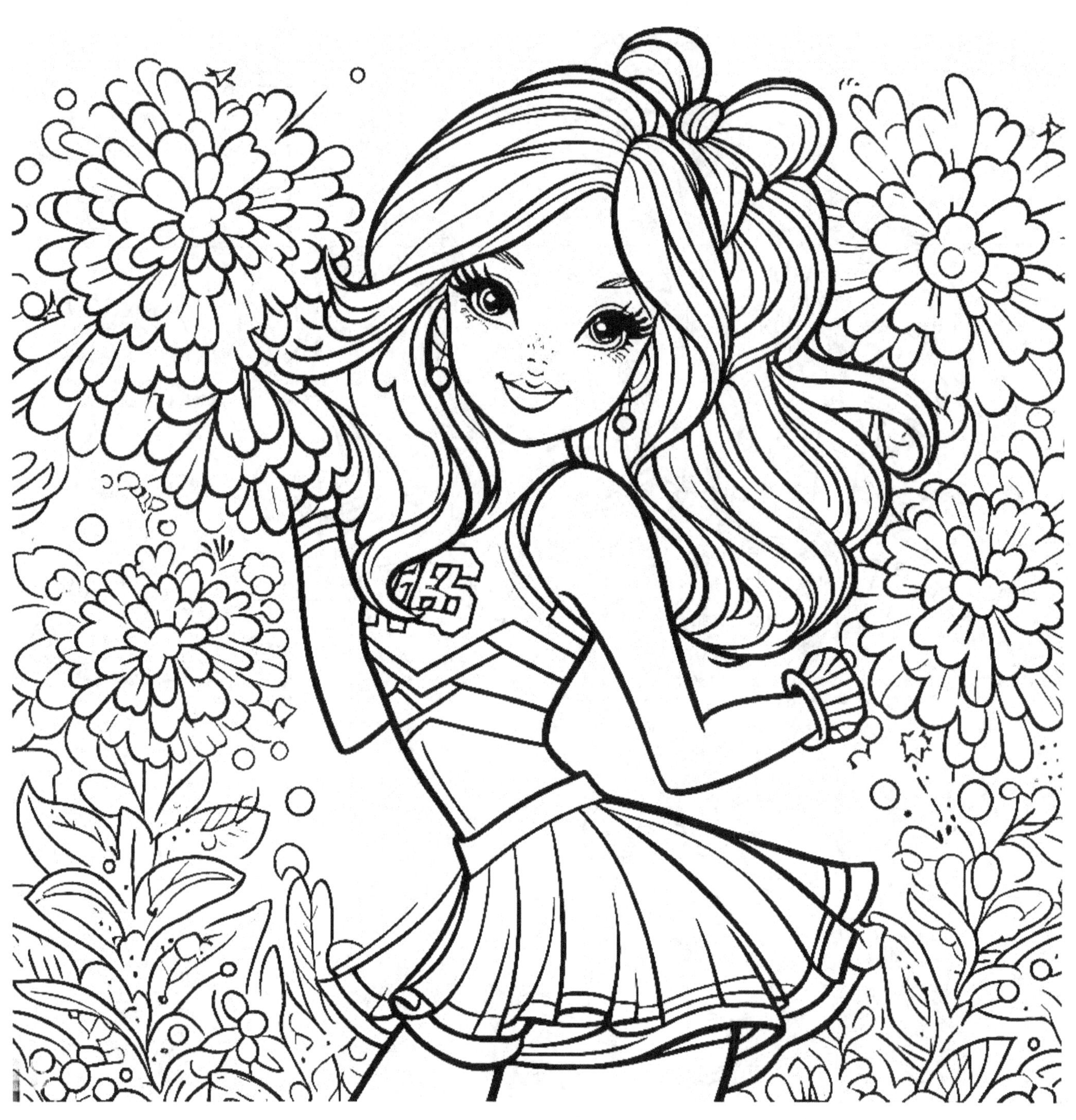

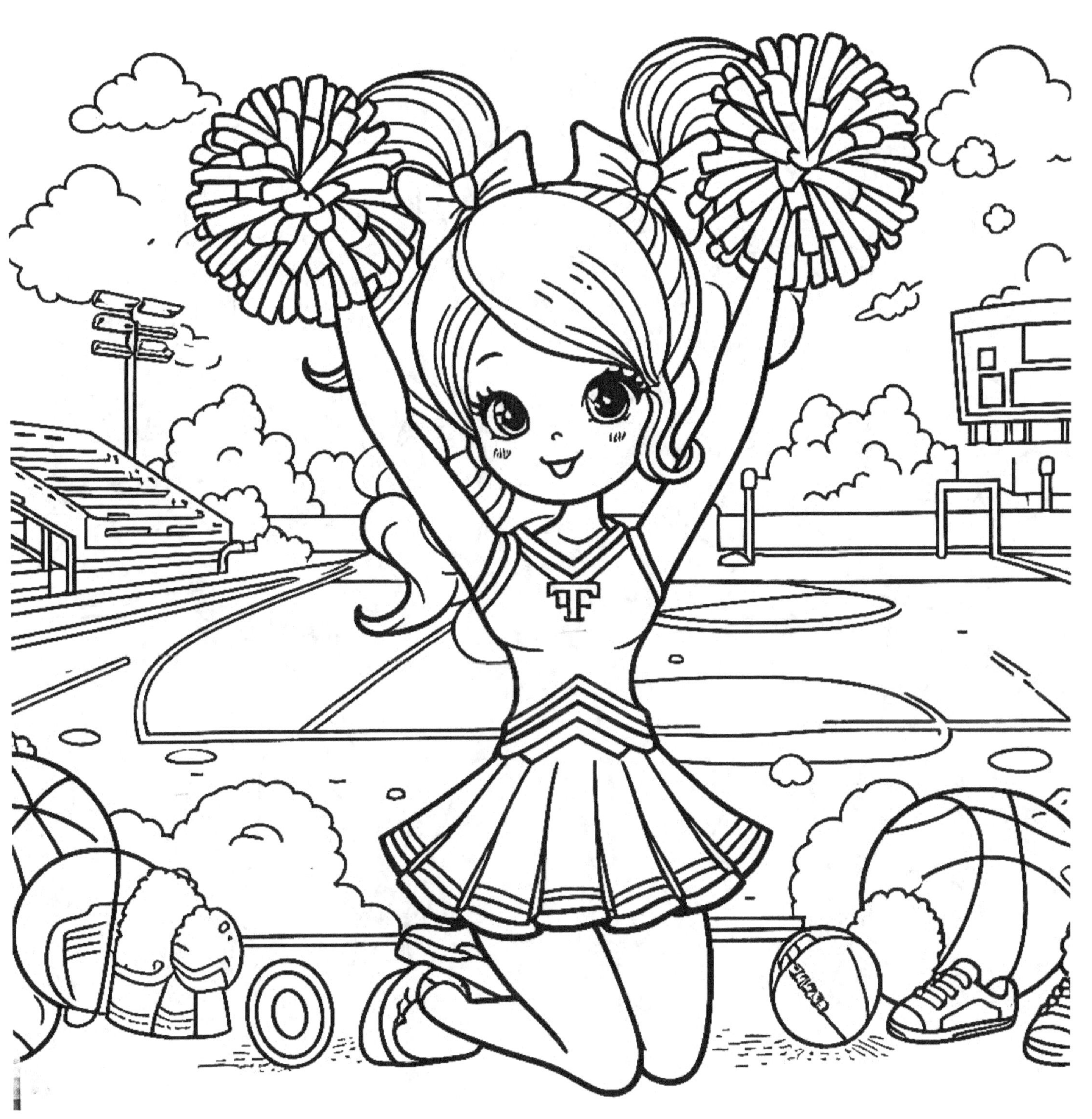

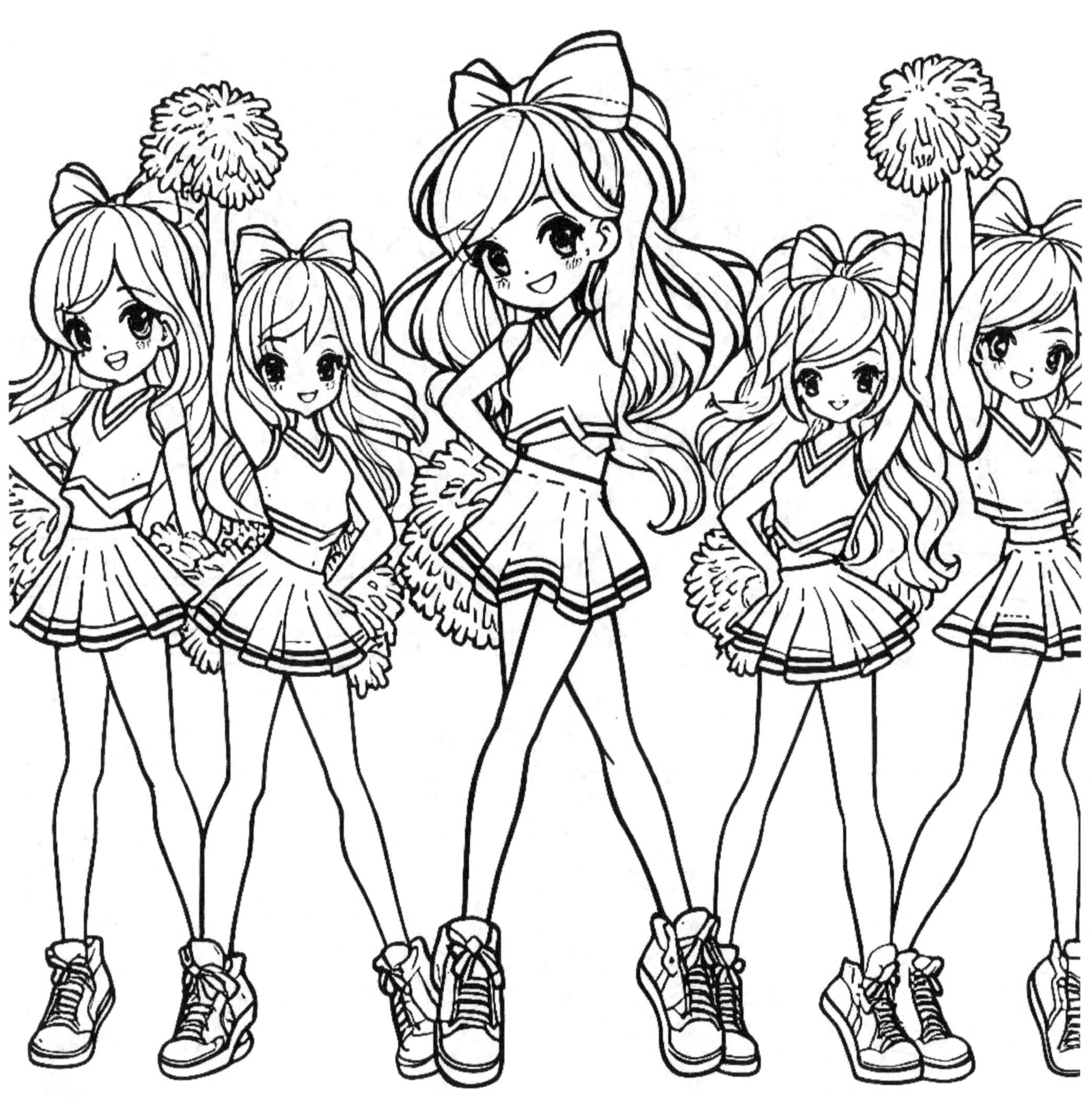

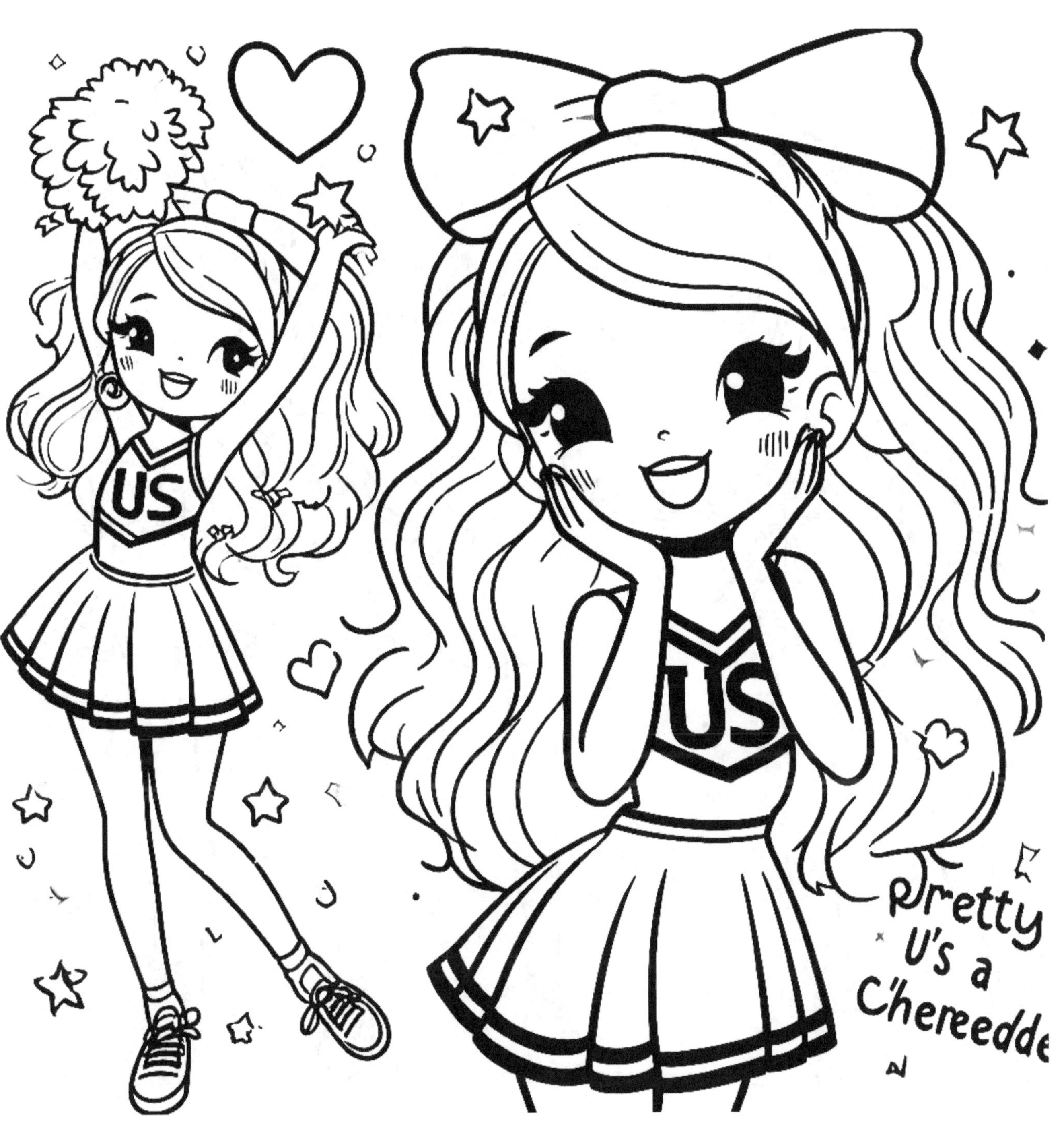

US
US
Pretty
U's a
Chereedde

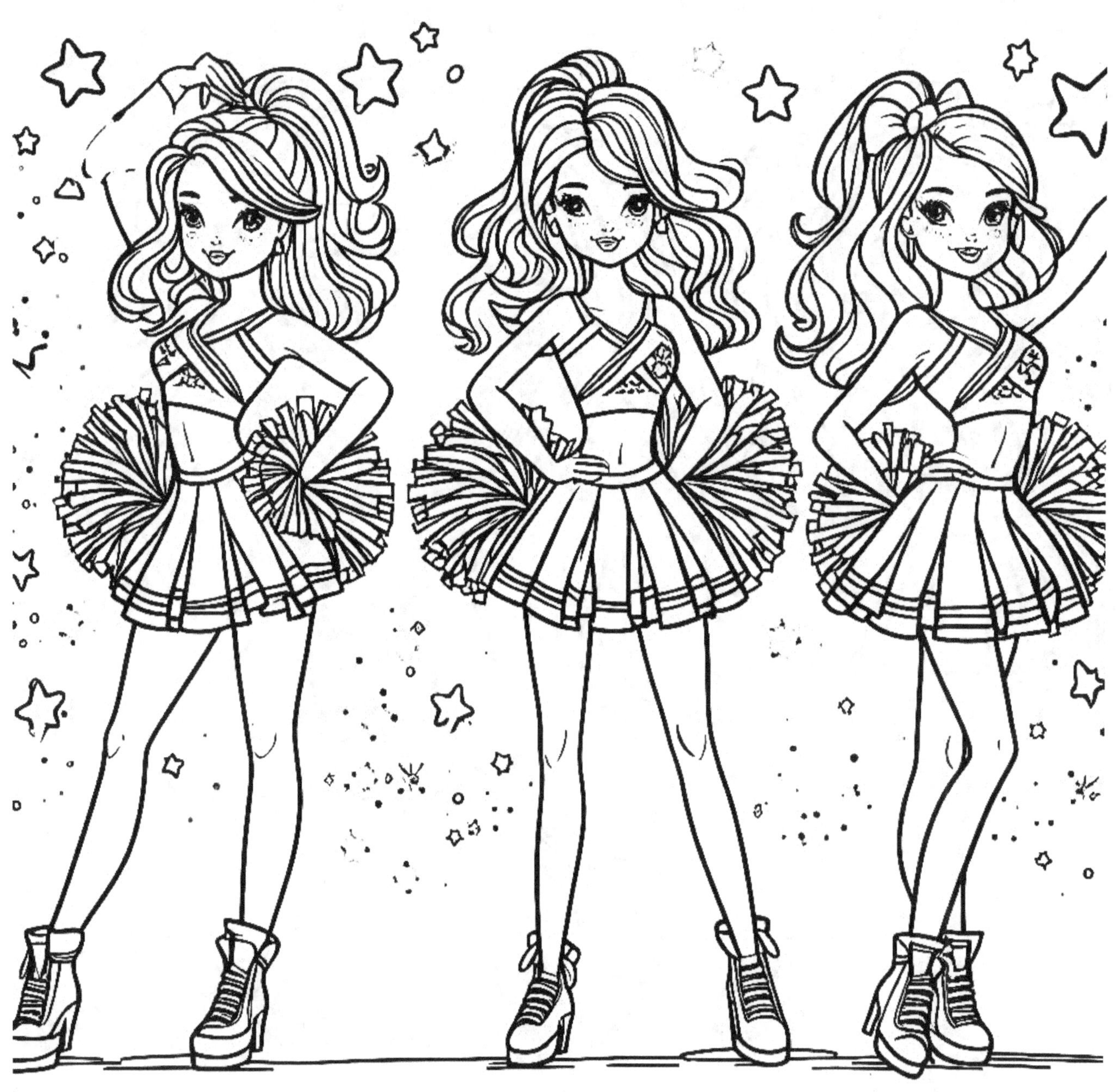

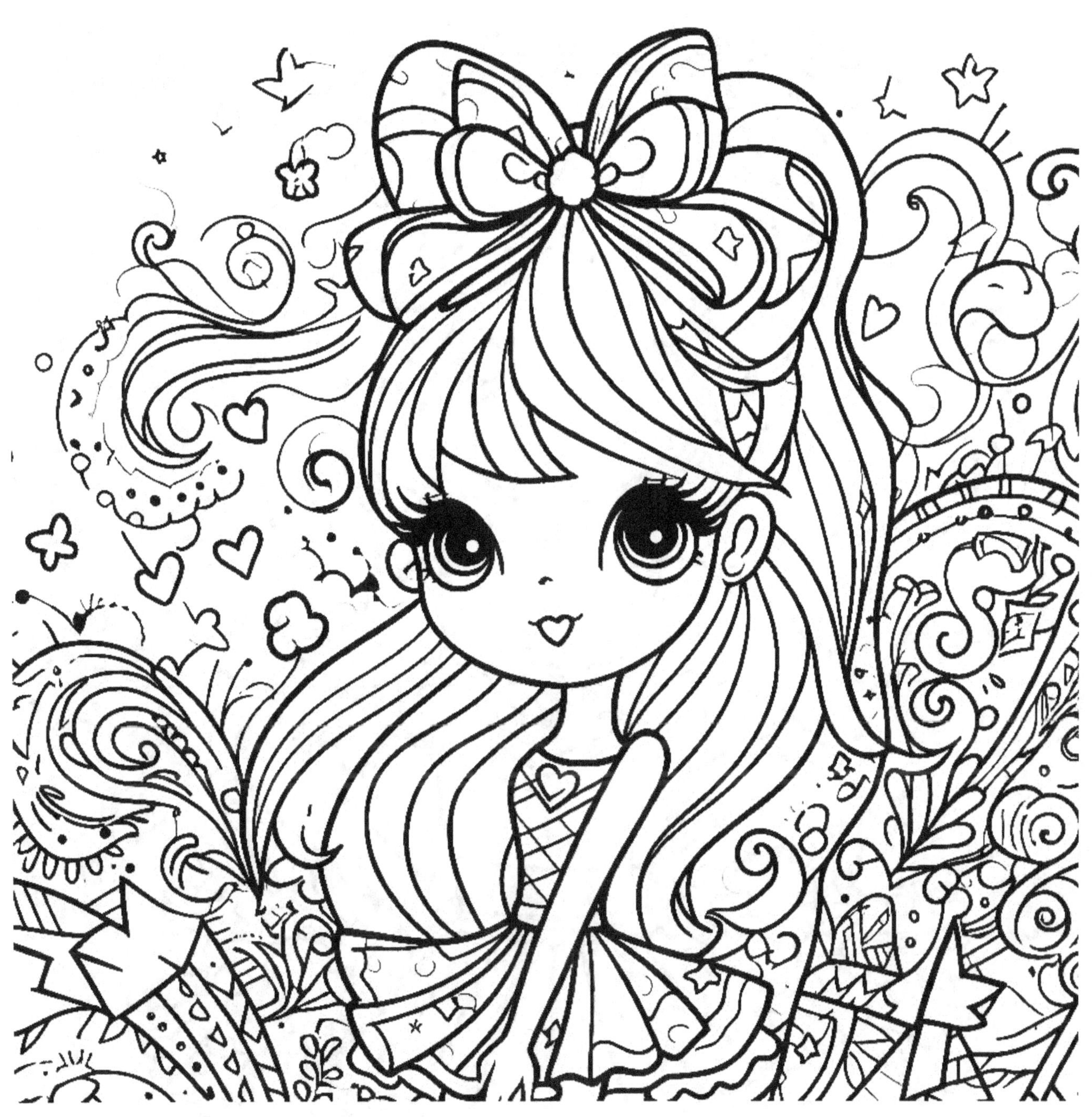

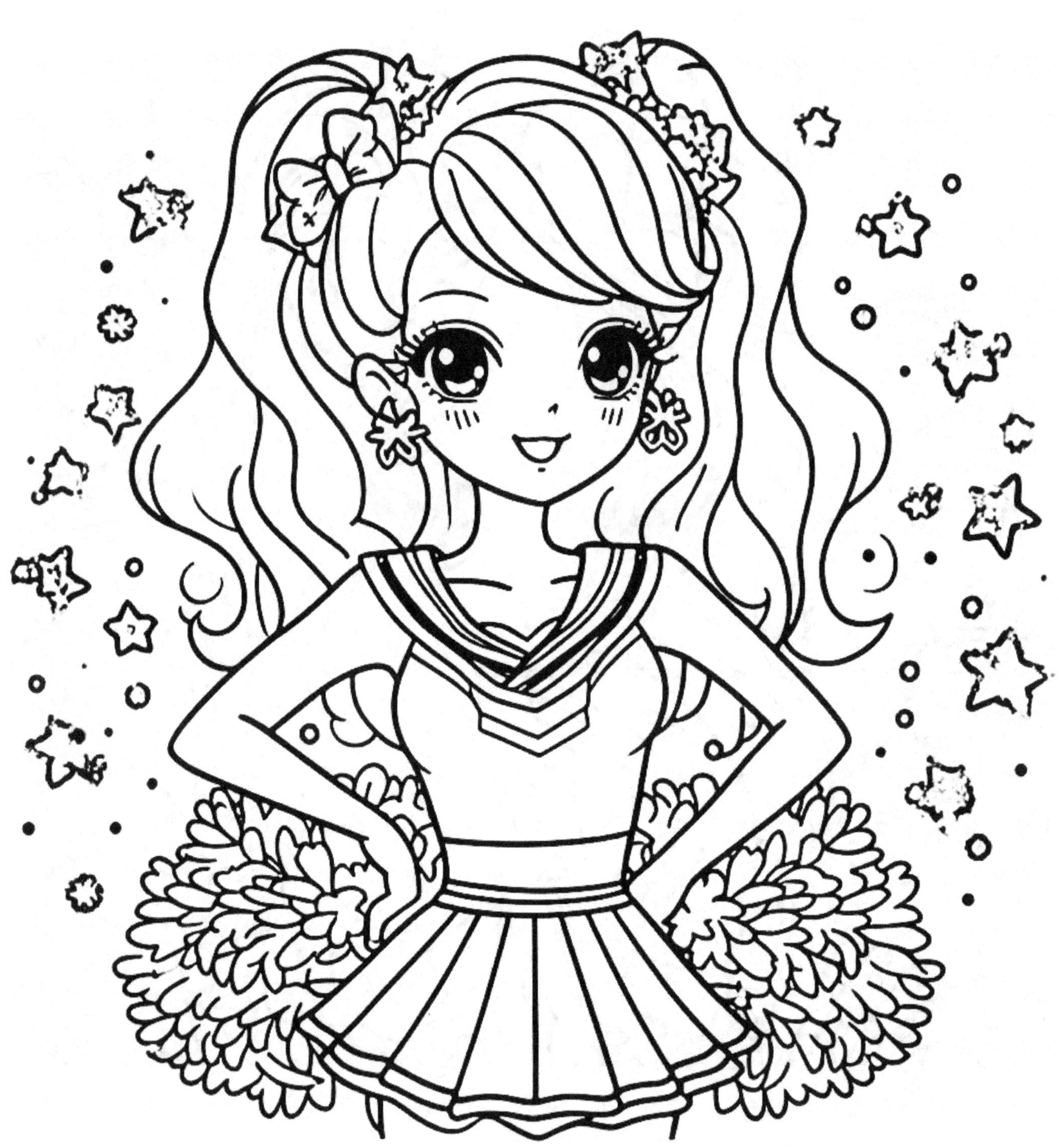

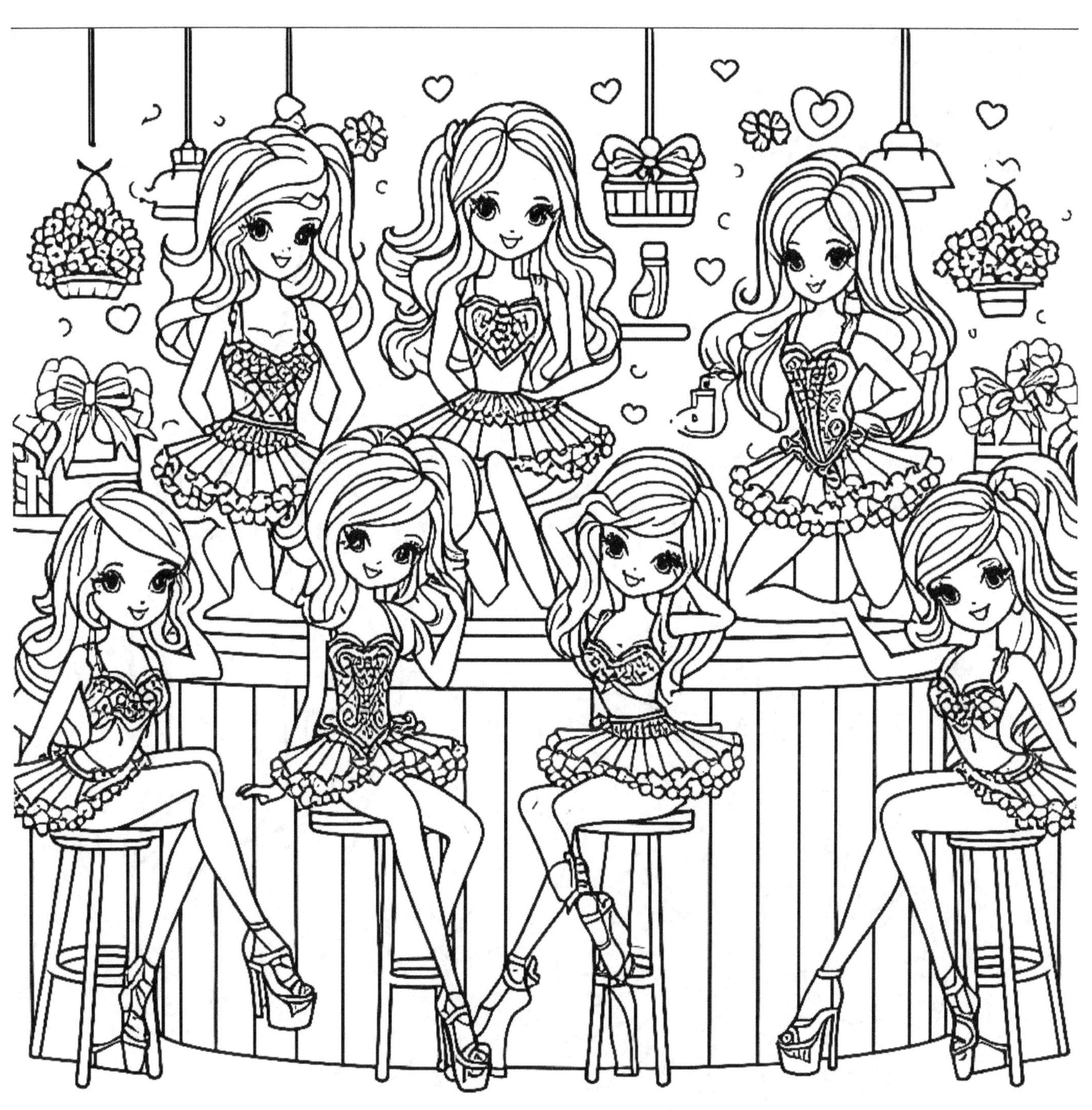

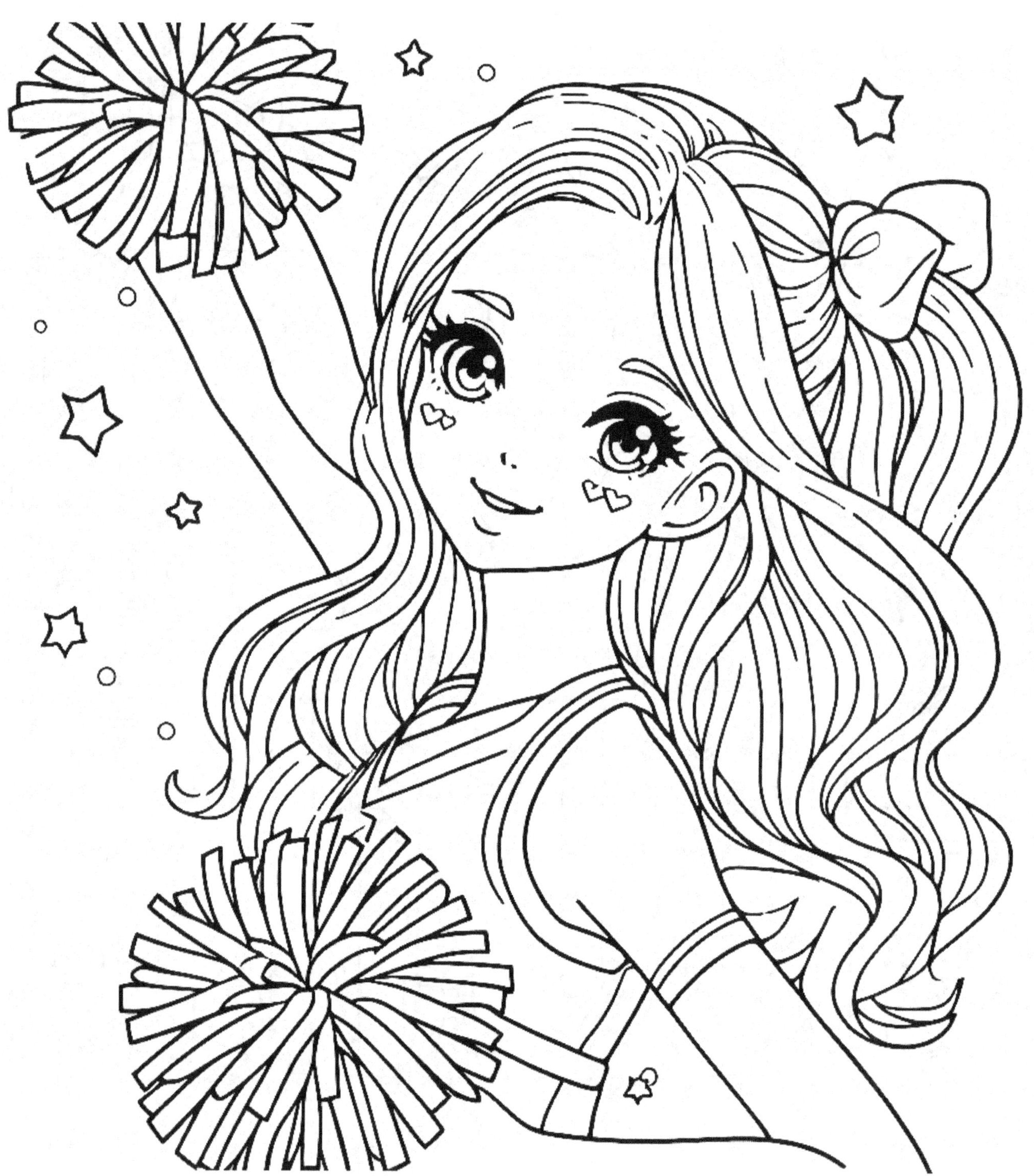

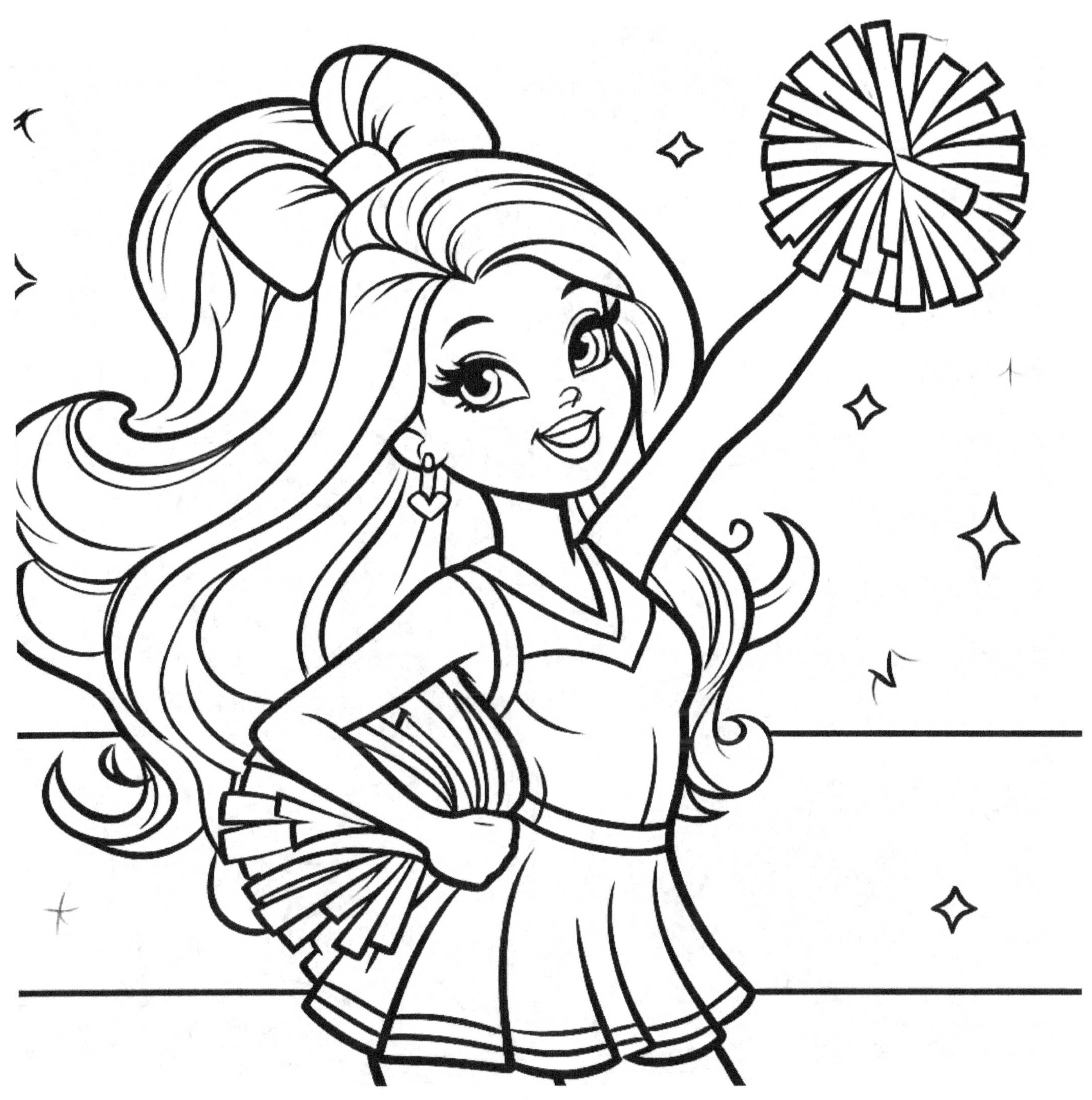

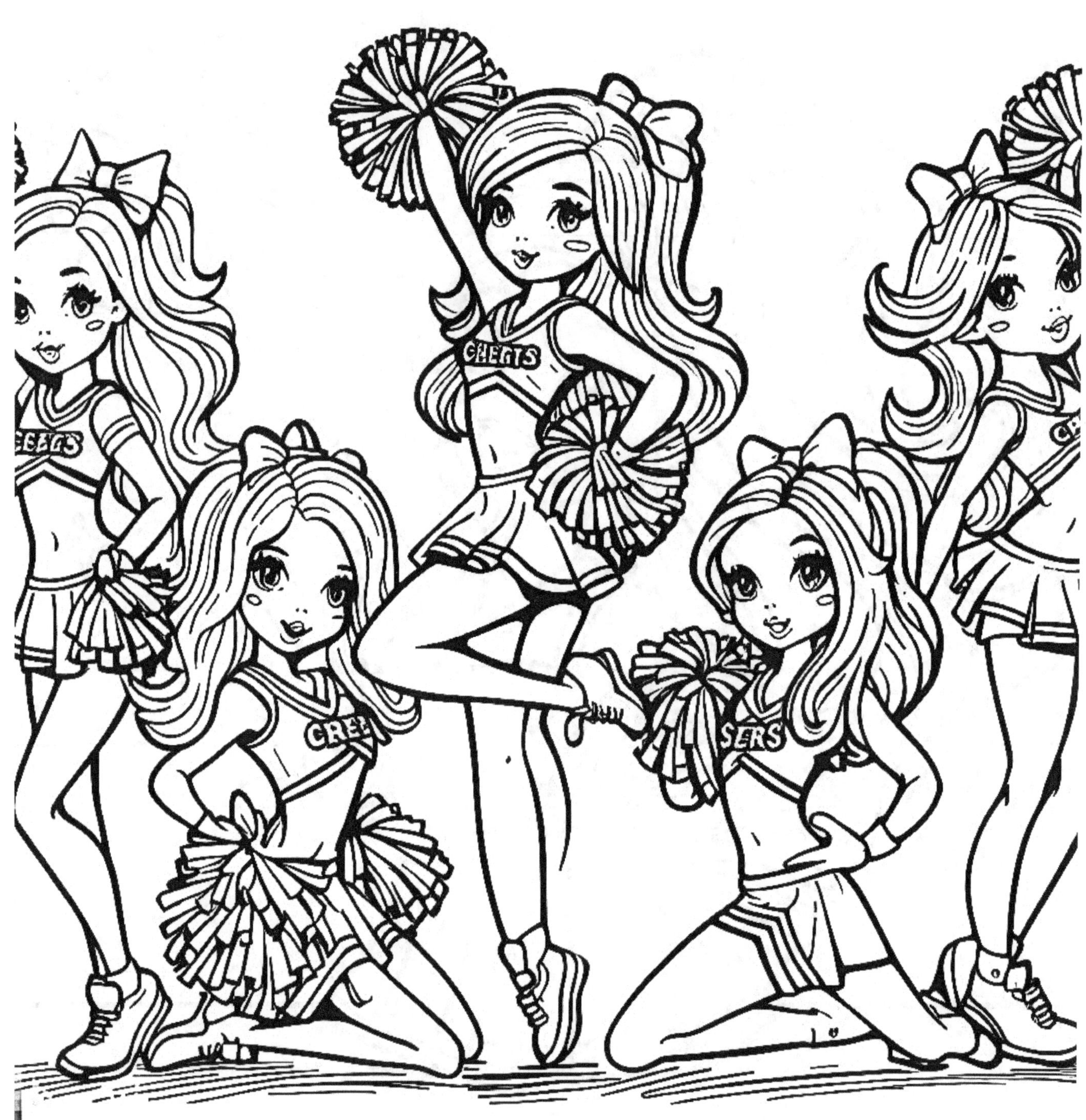

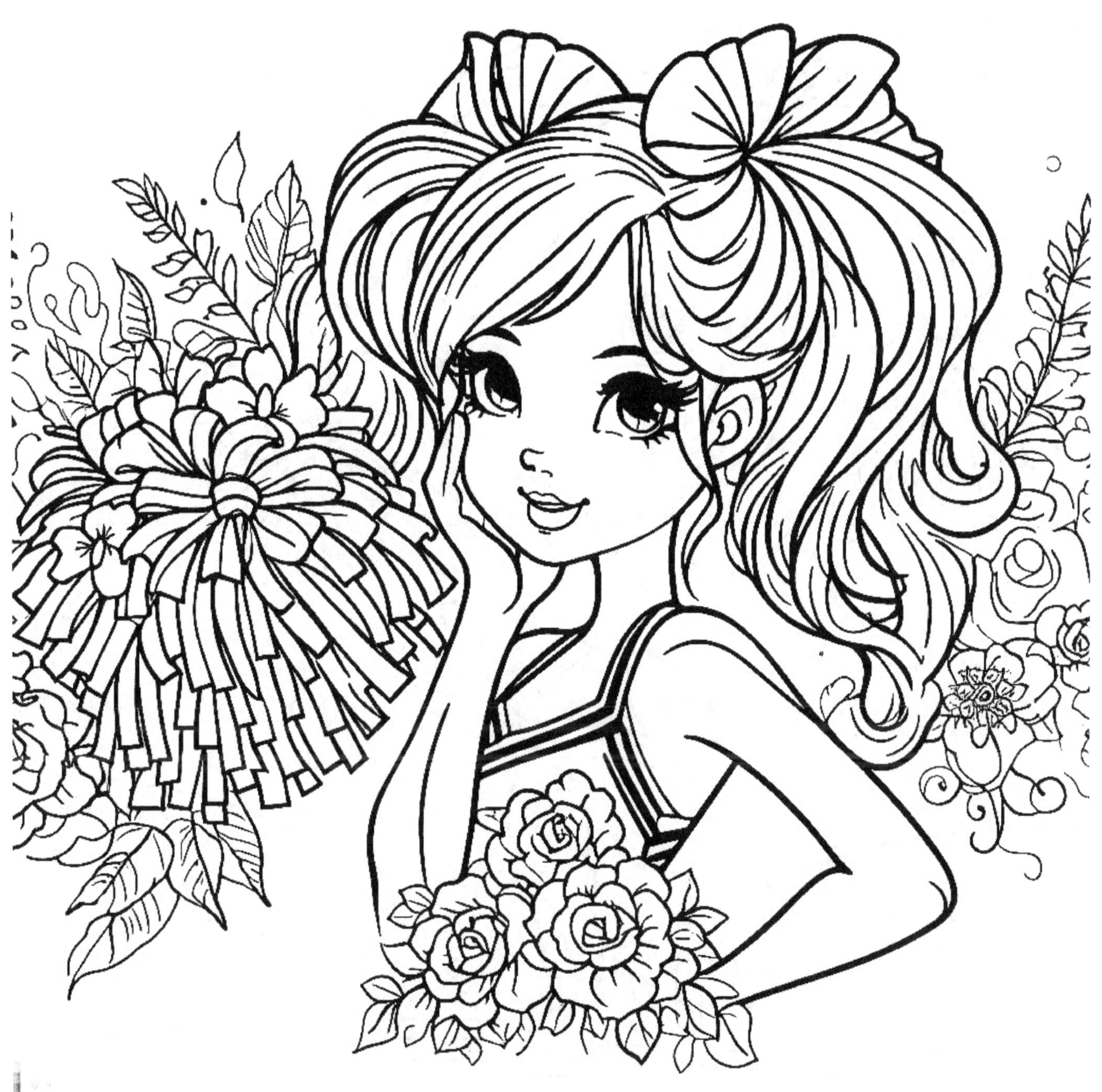

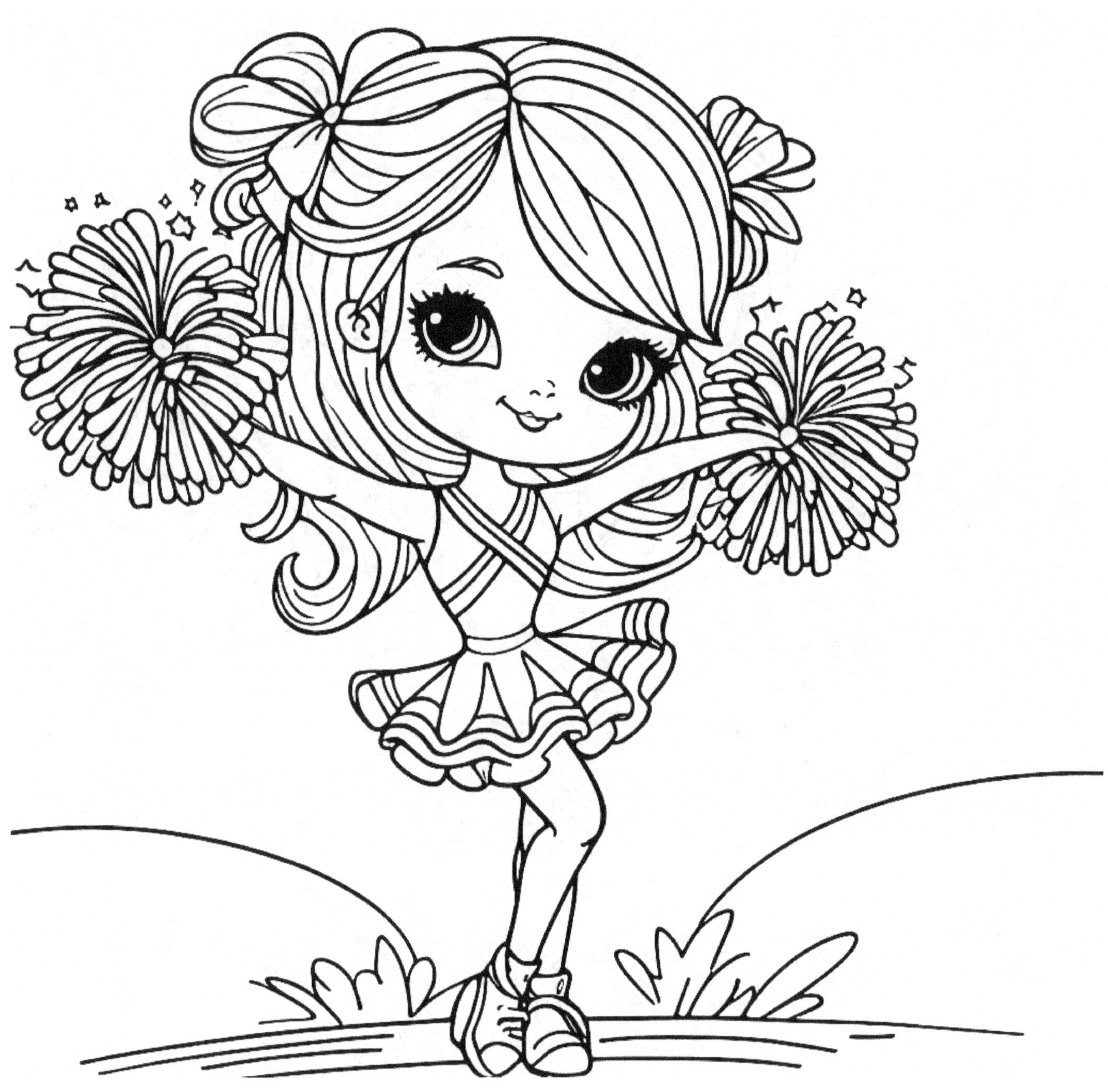

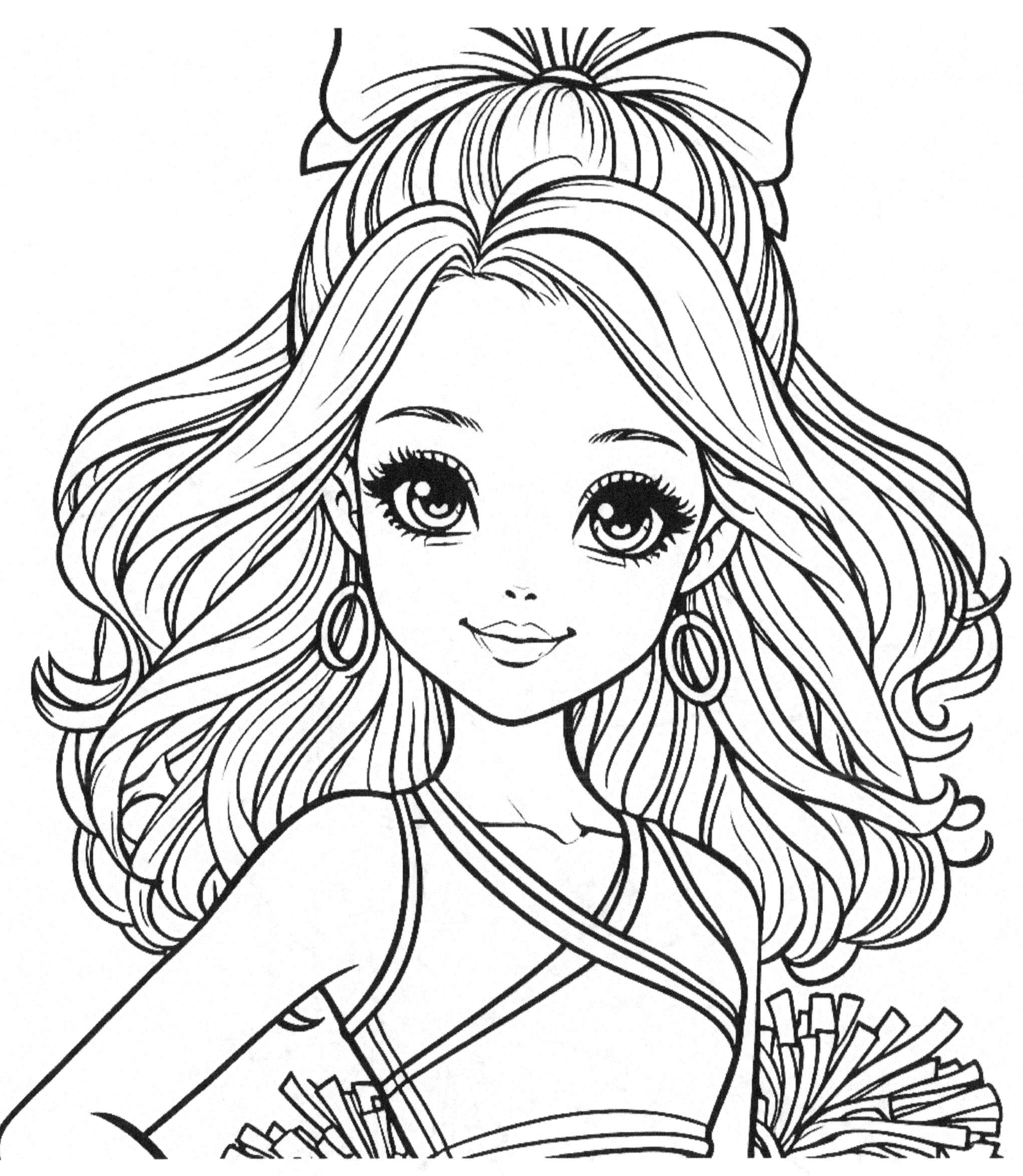

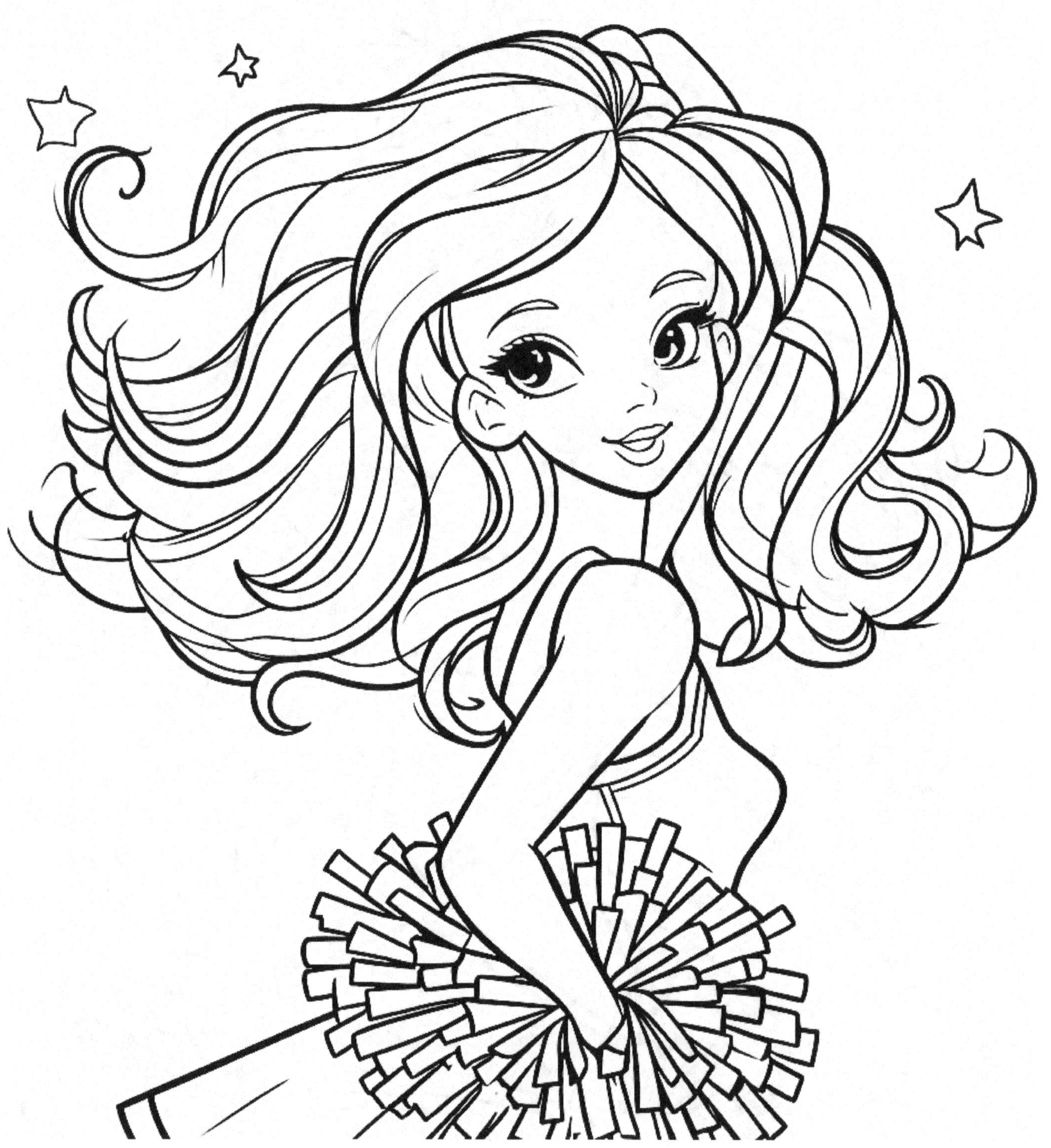

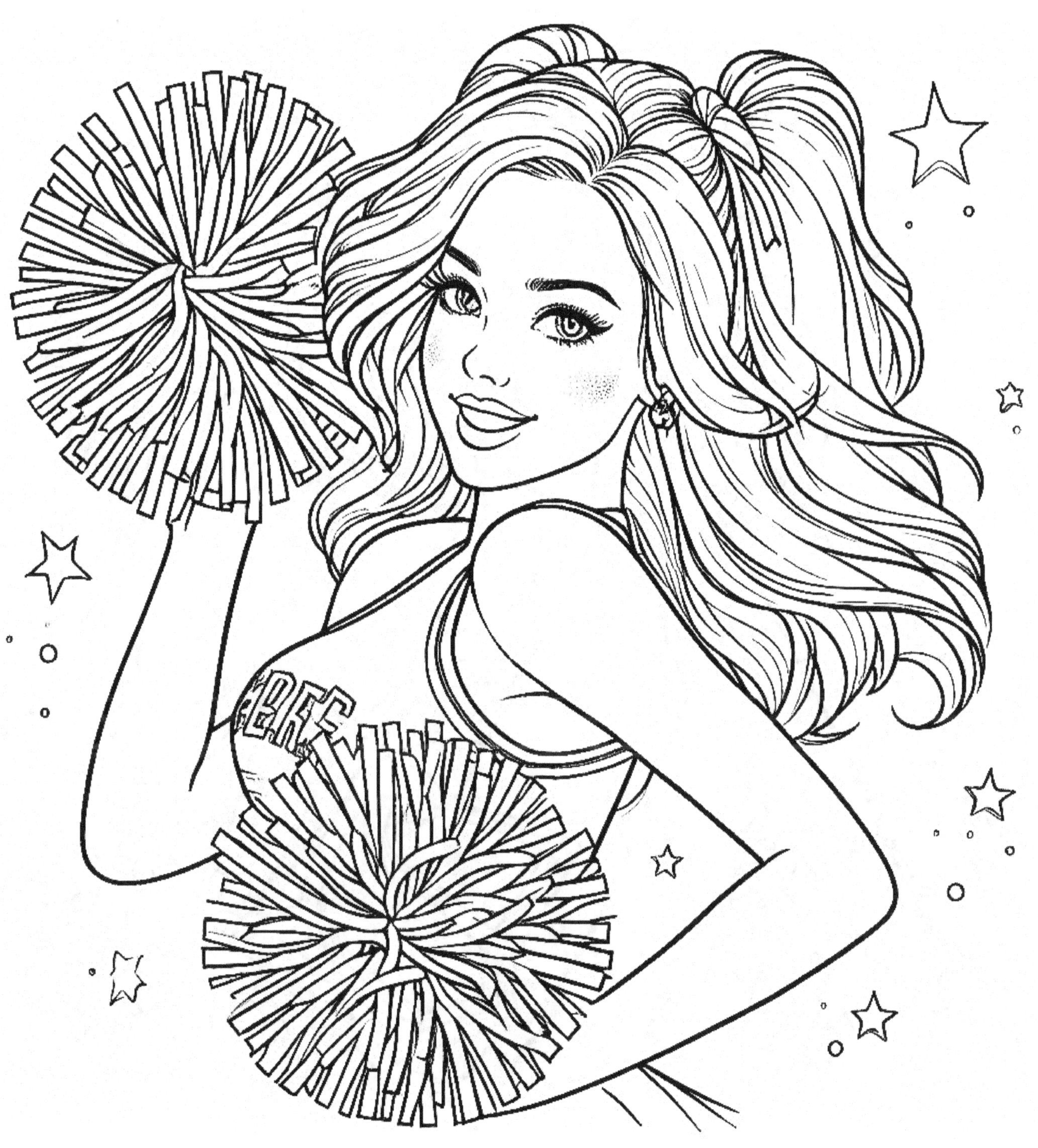

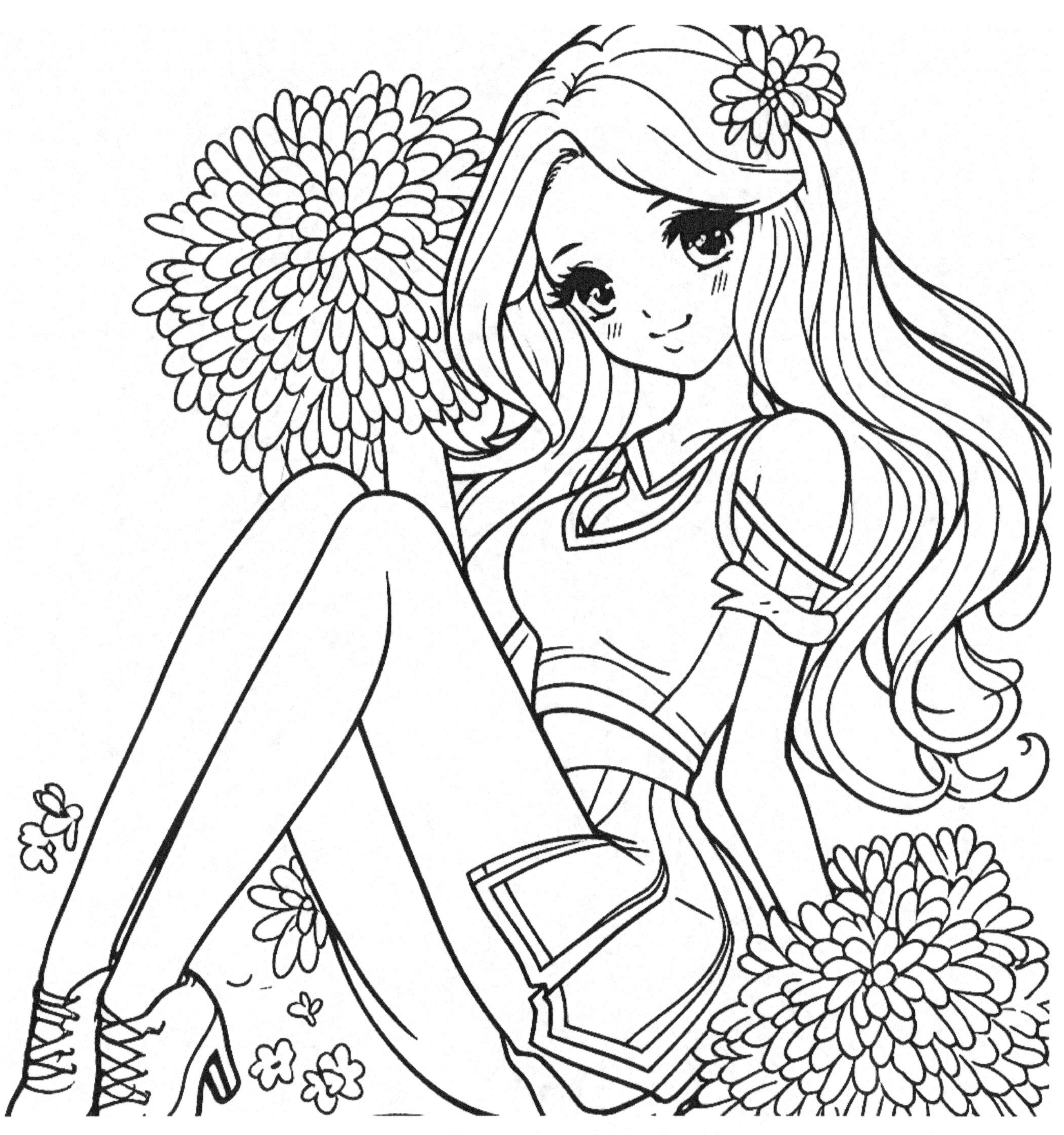

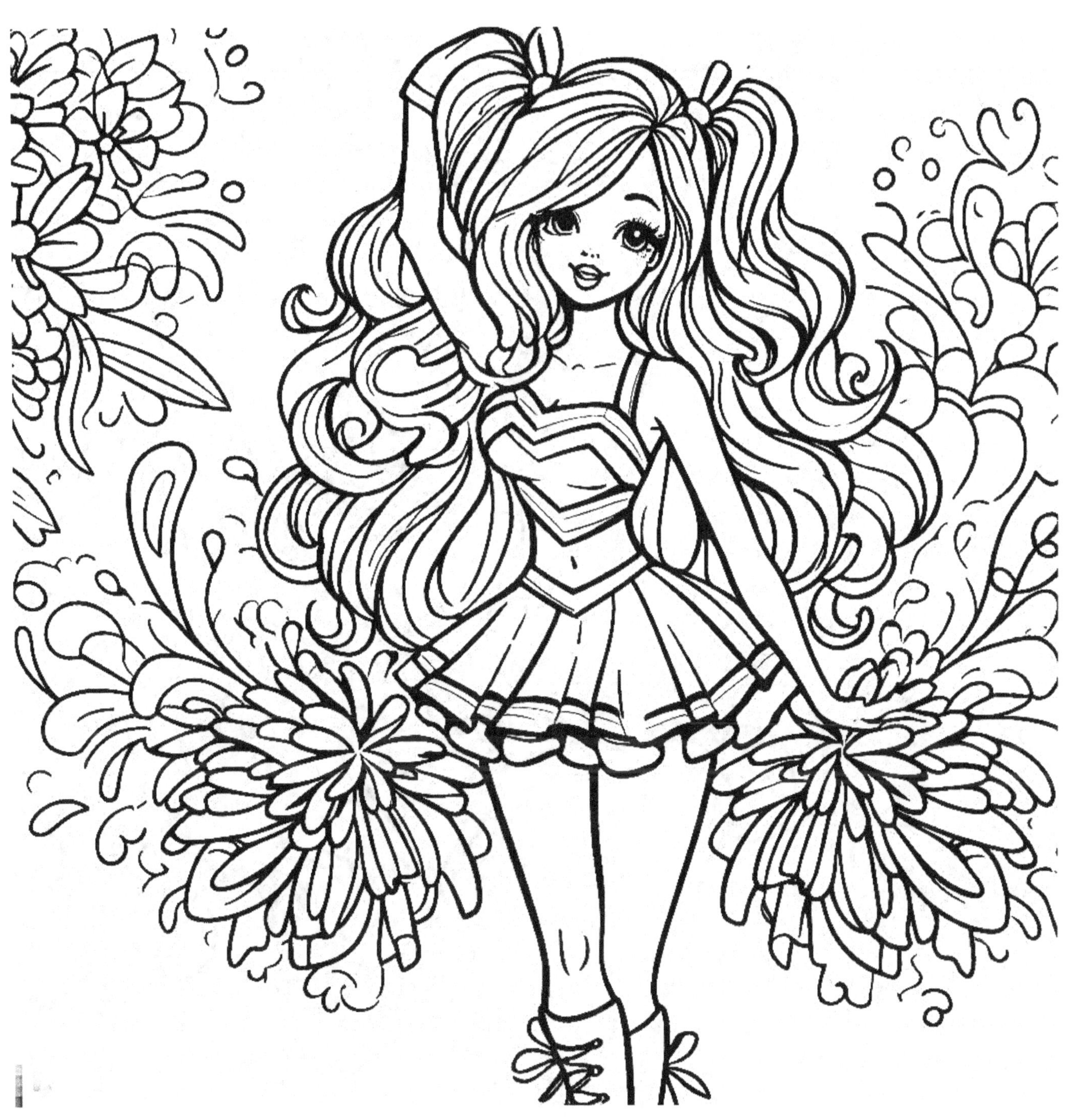

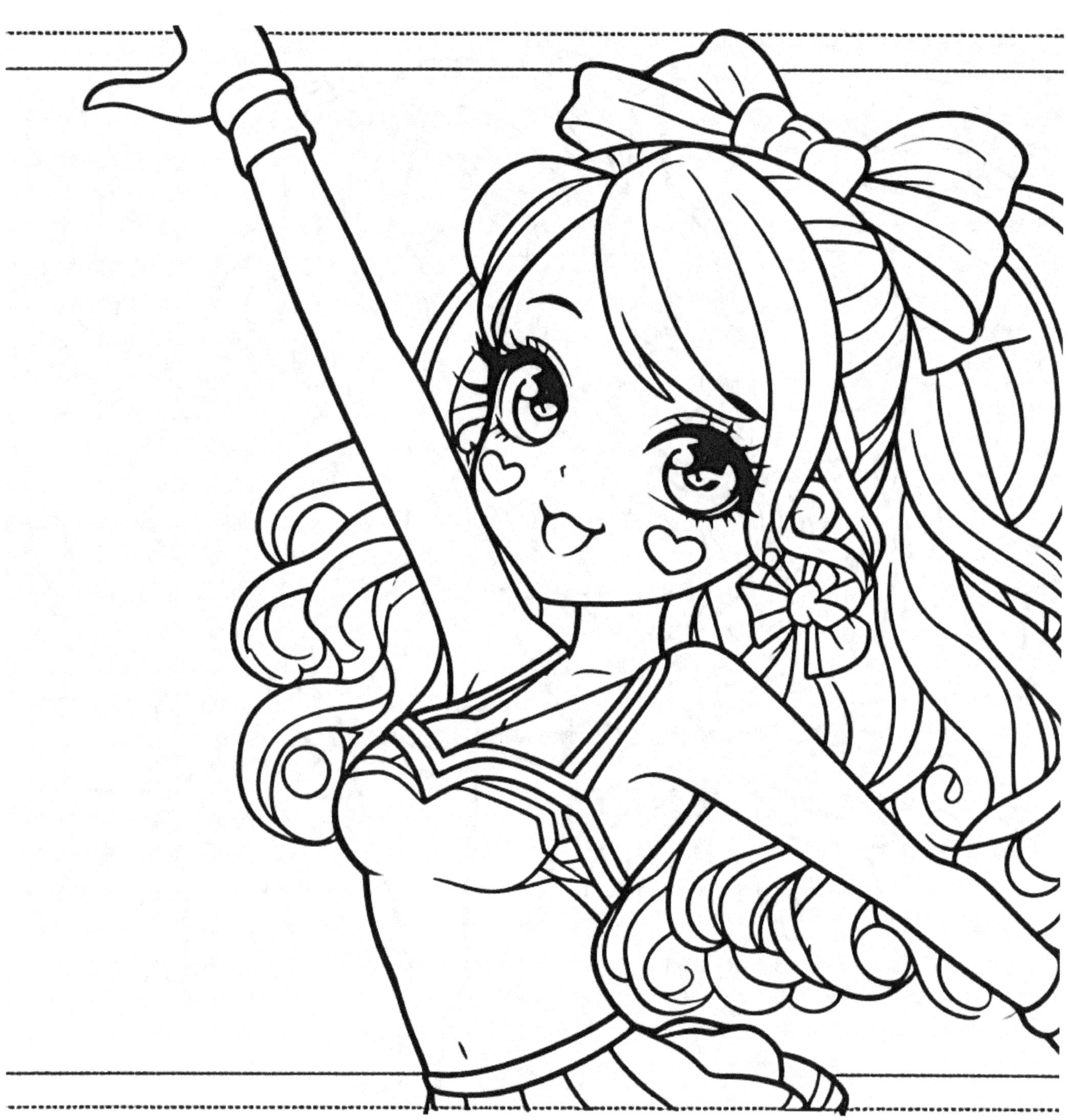

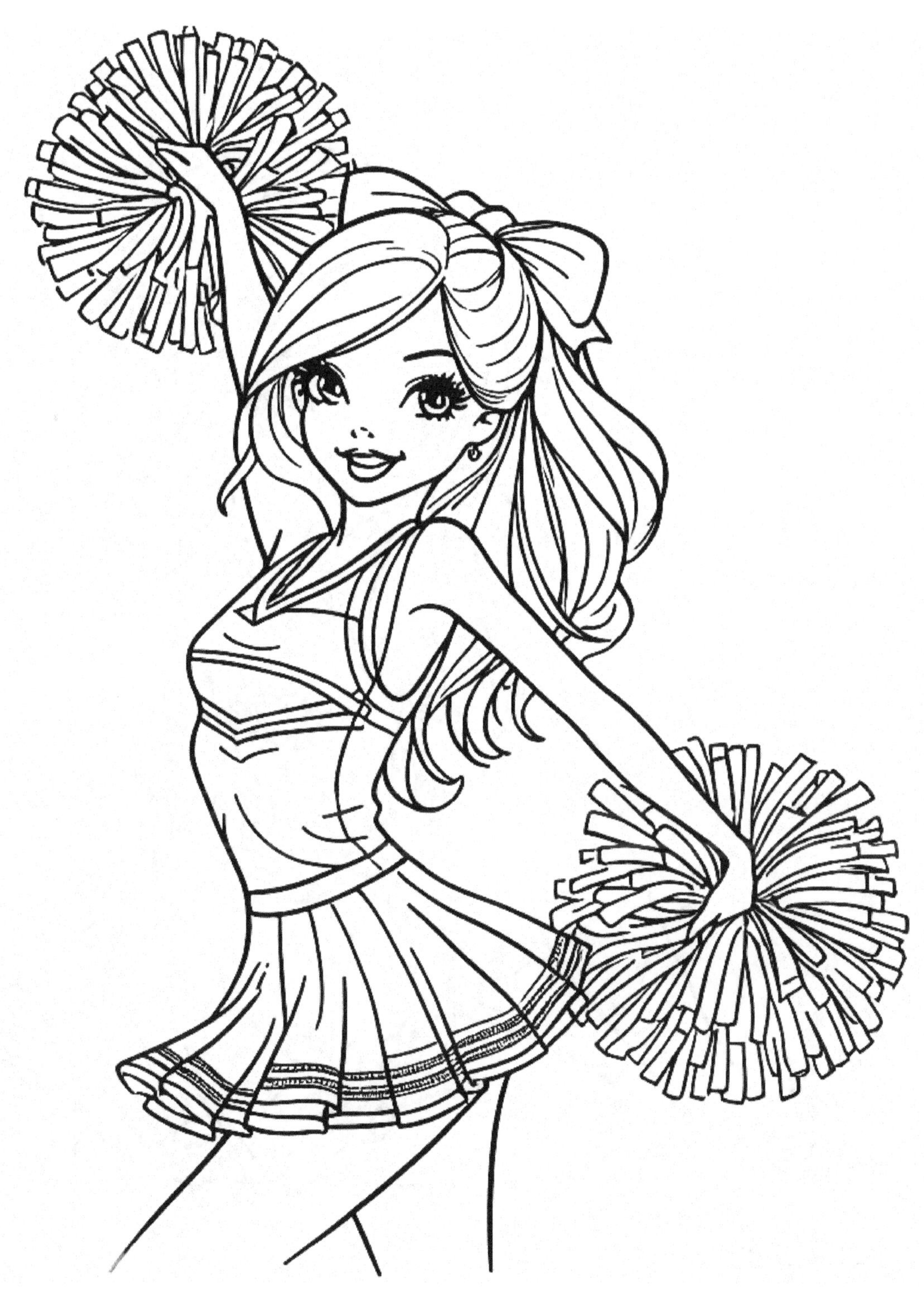

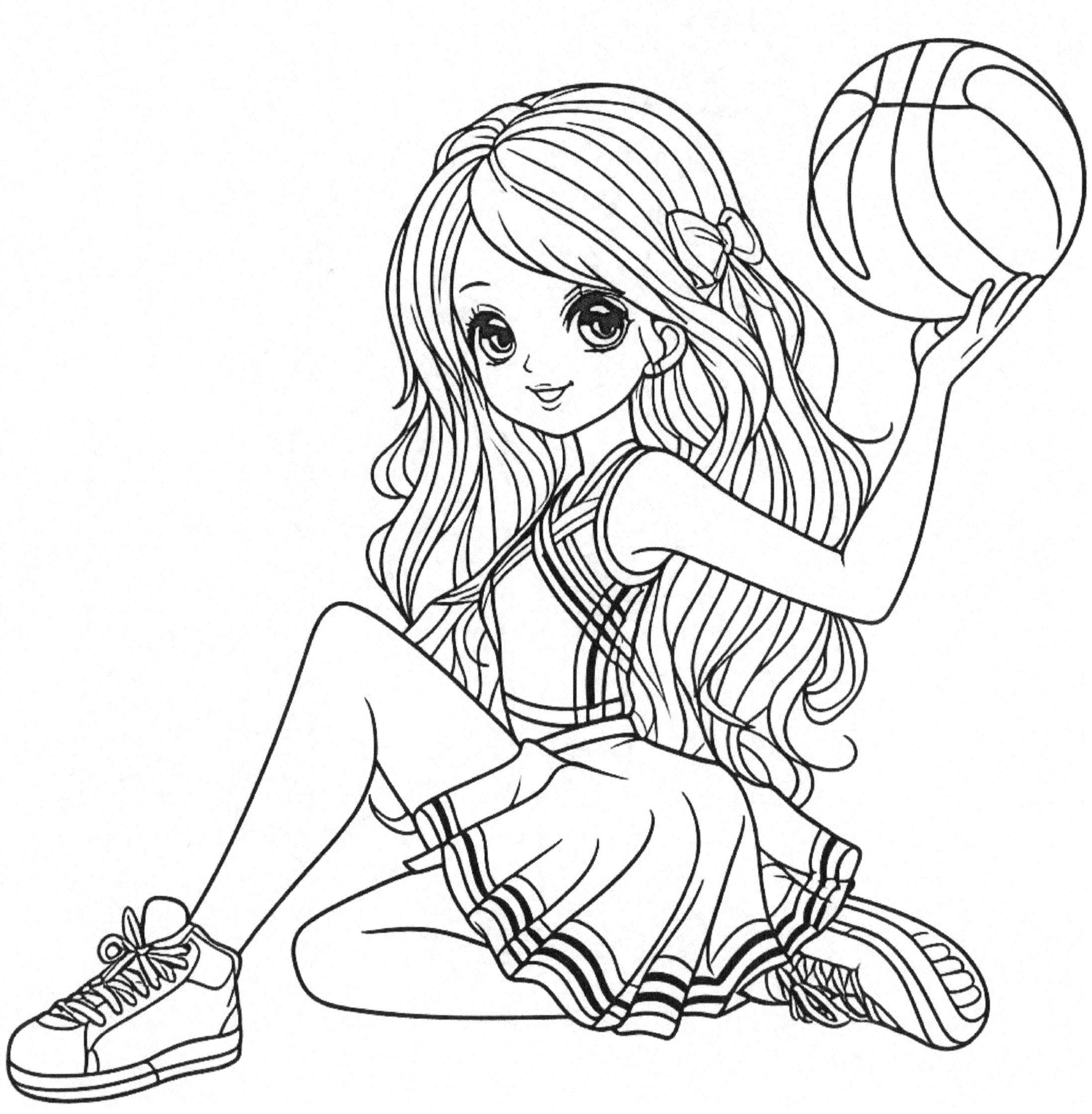

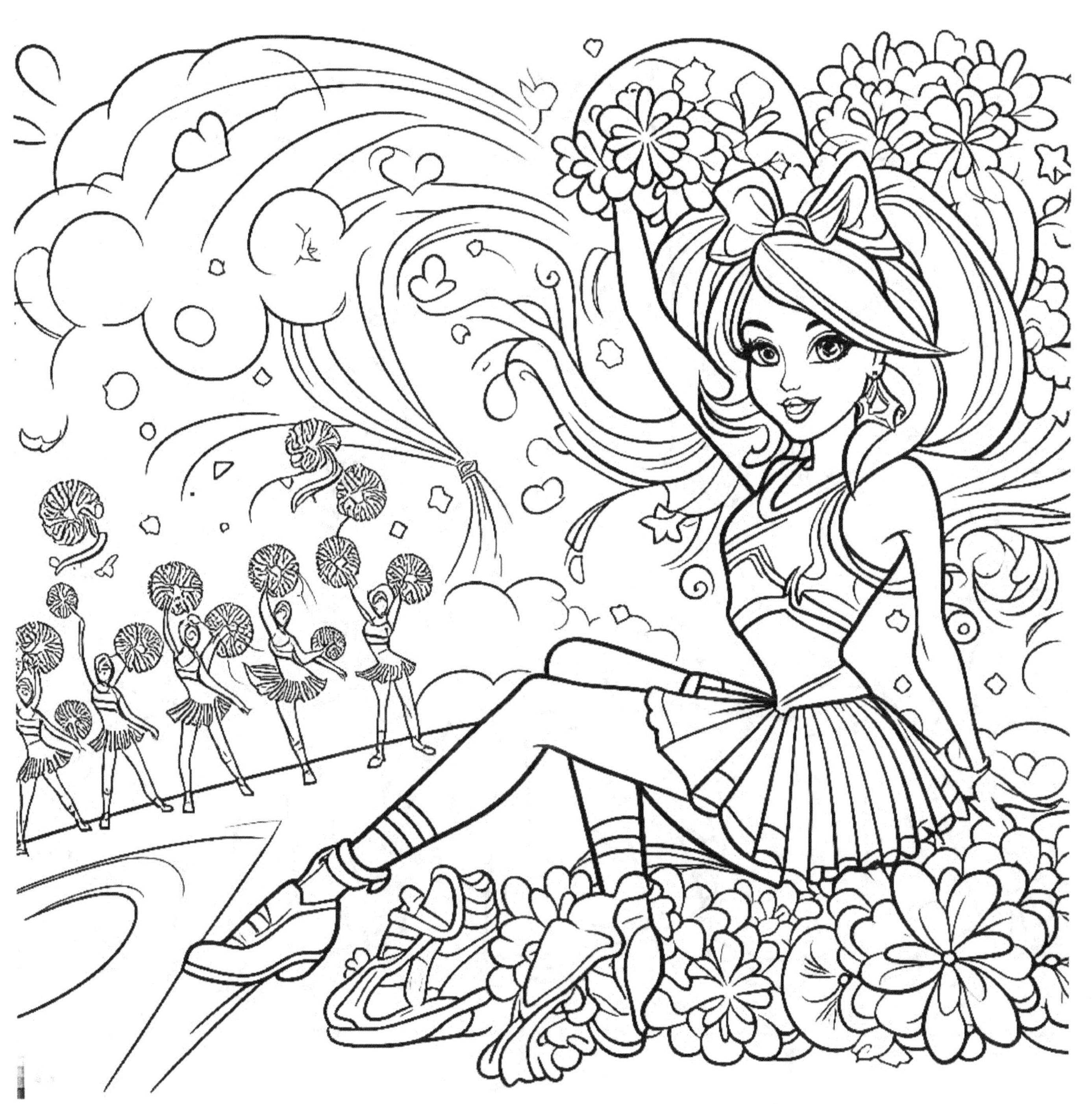

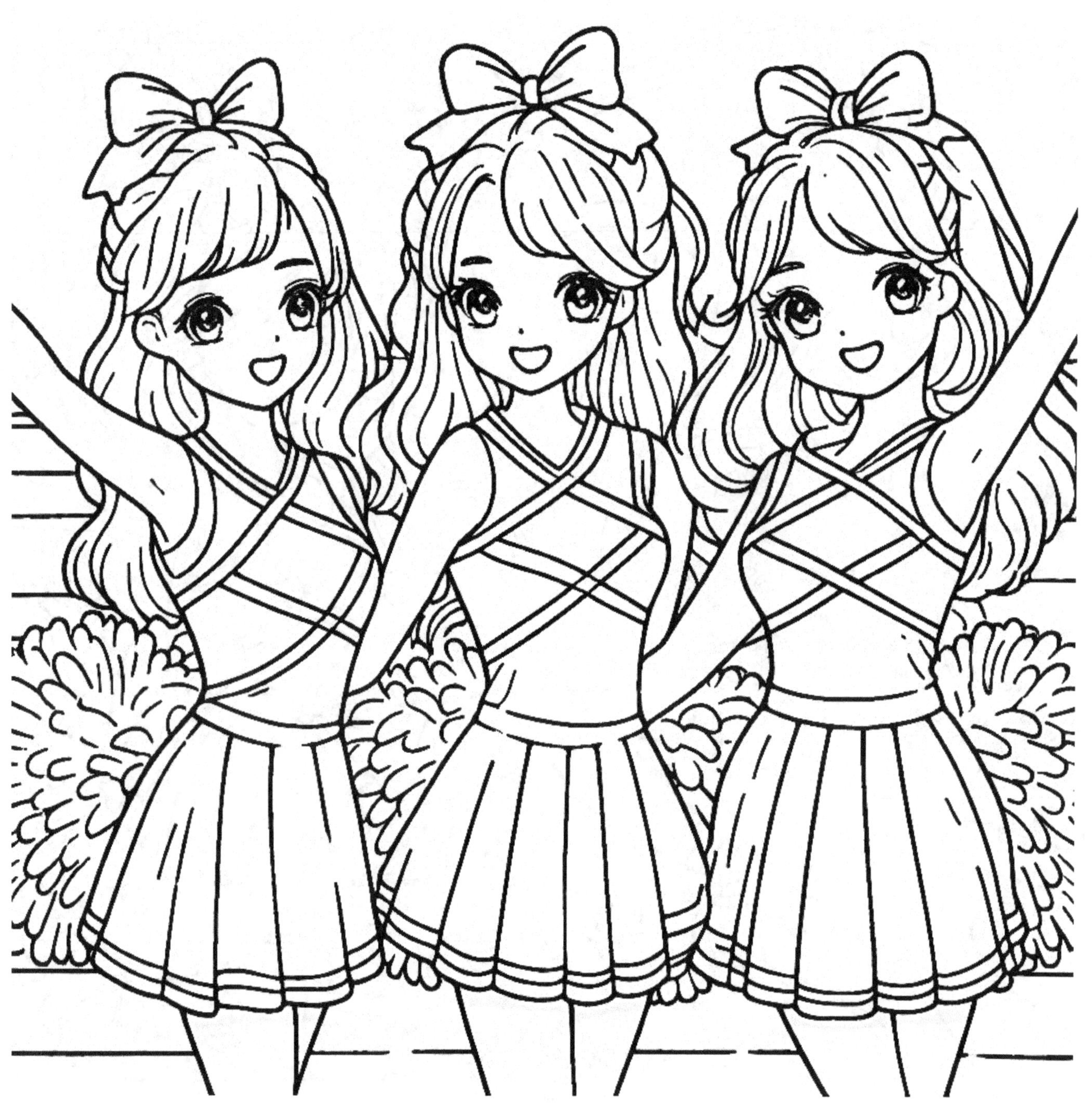

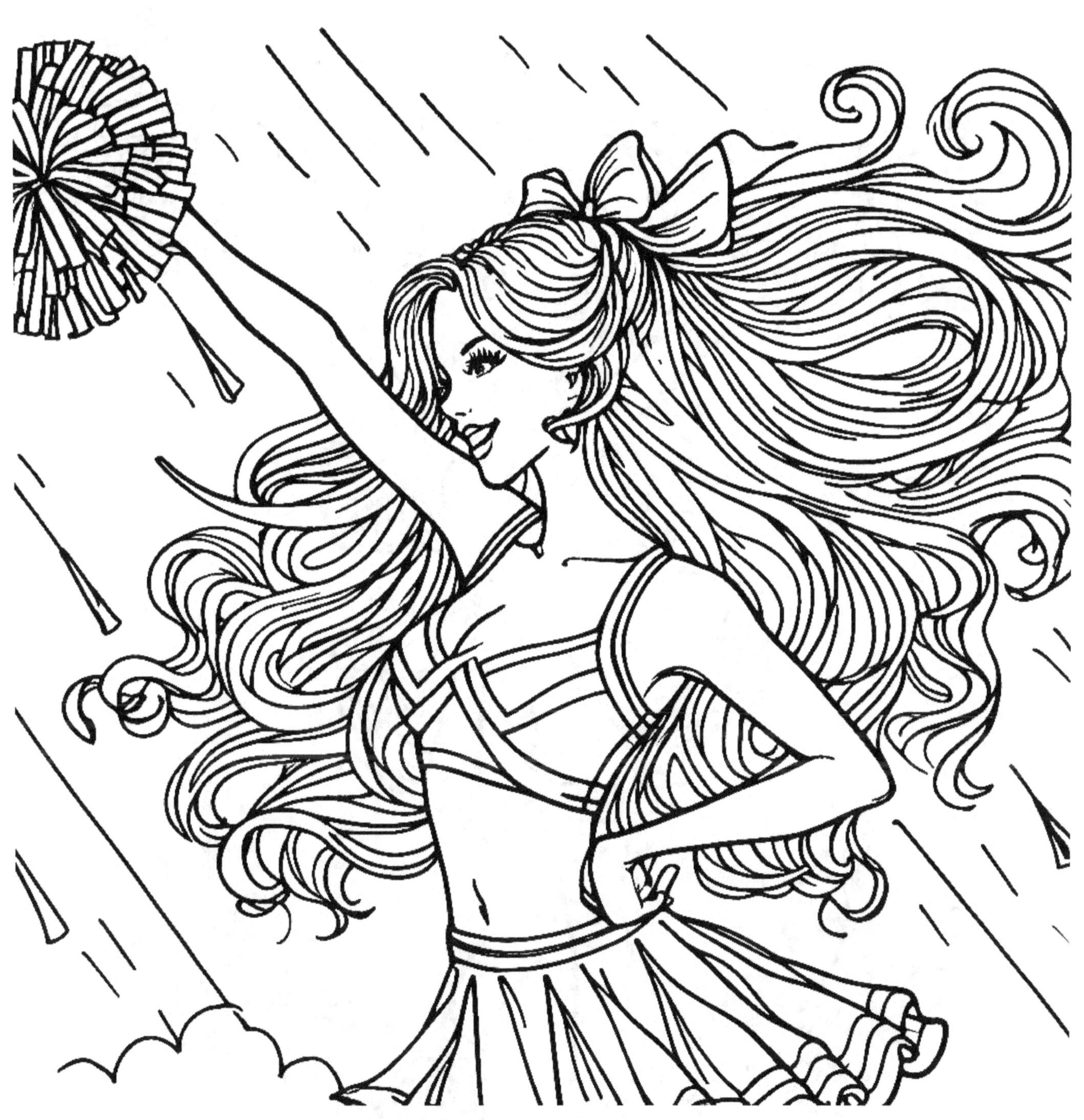

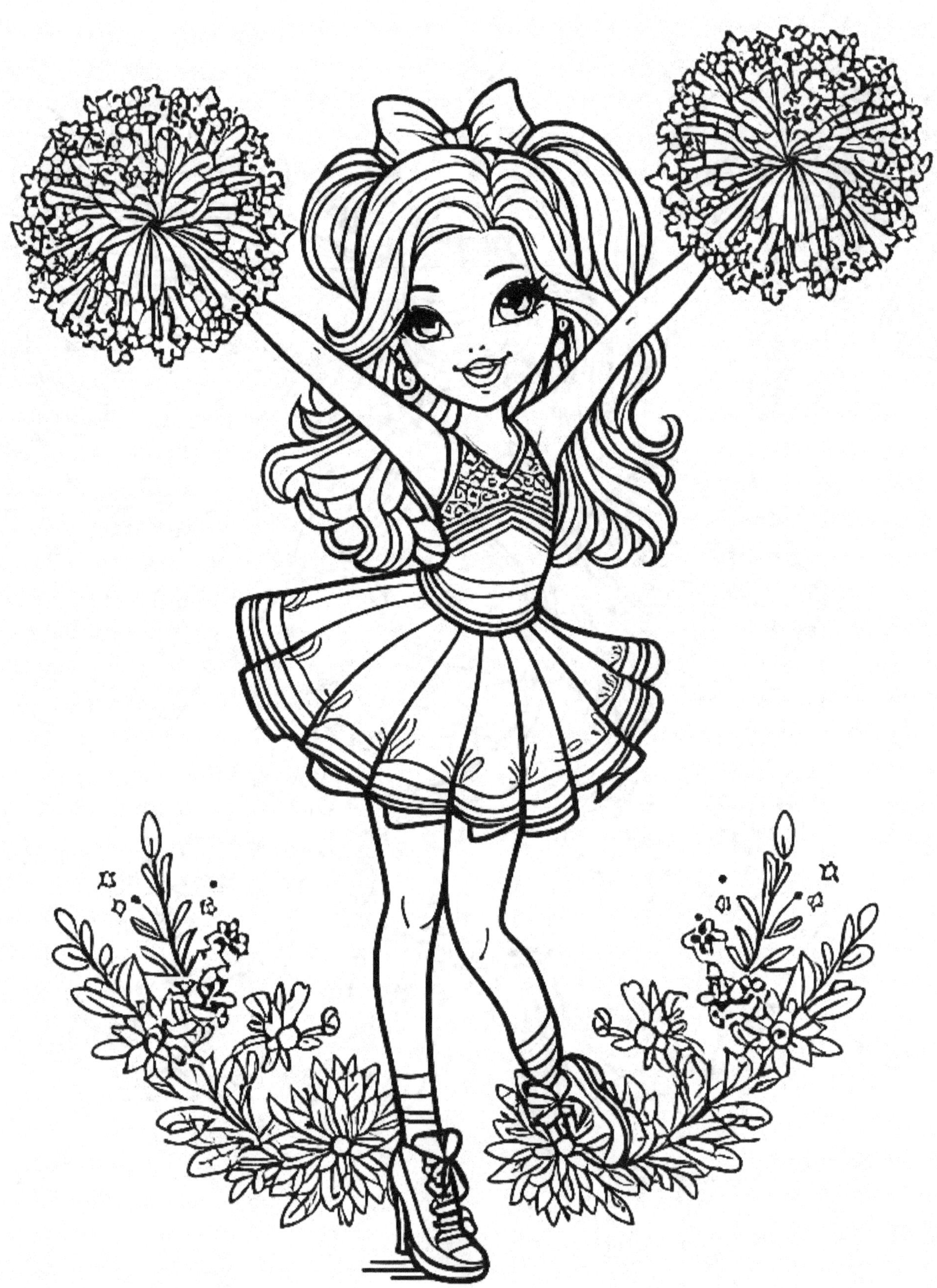

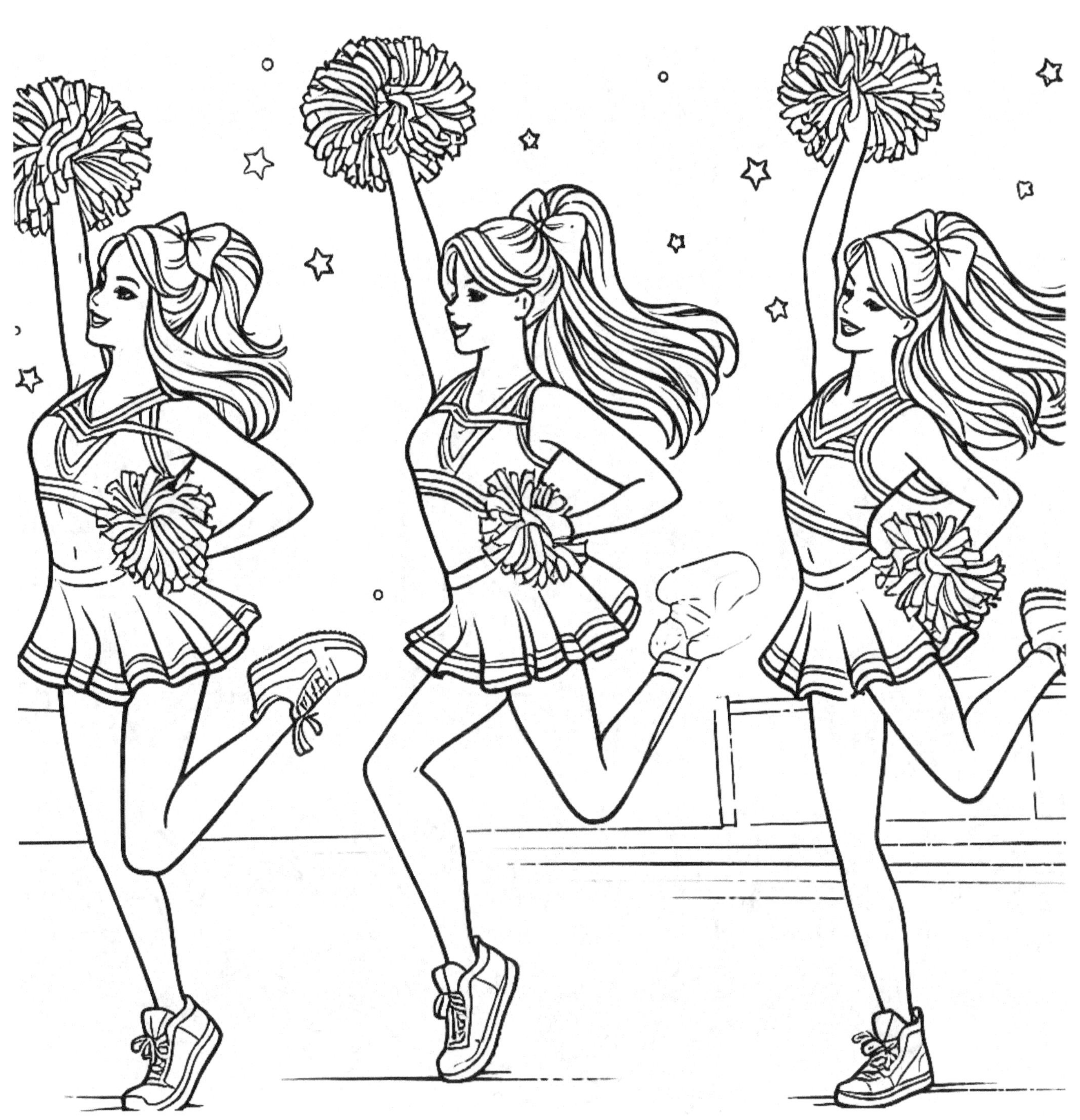

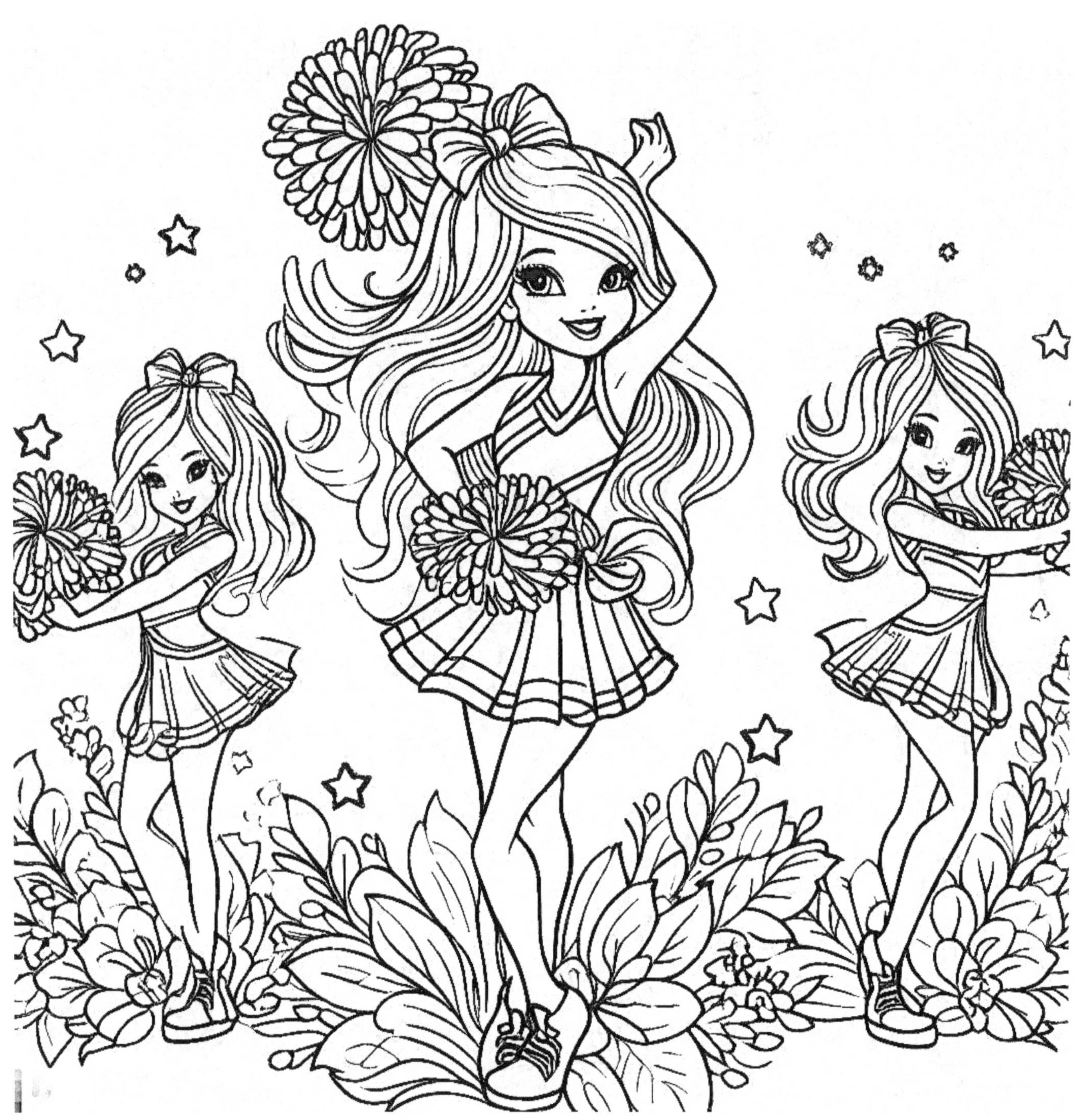

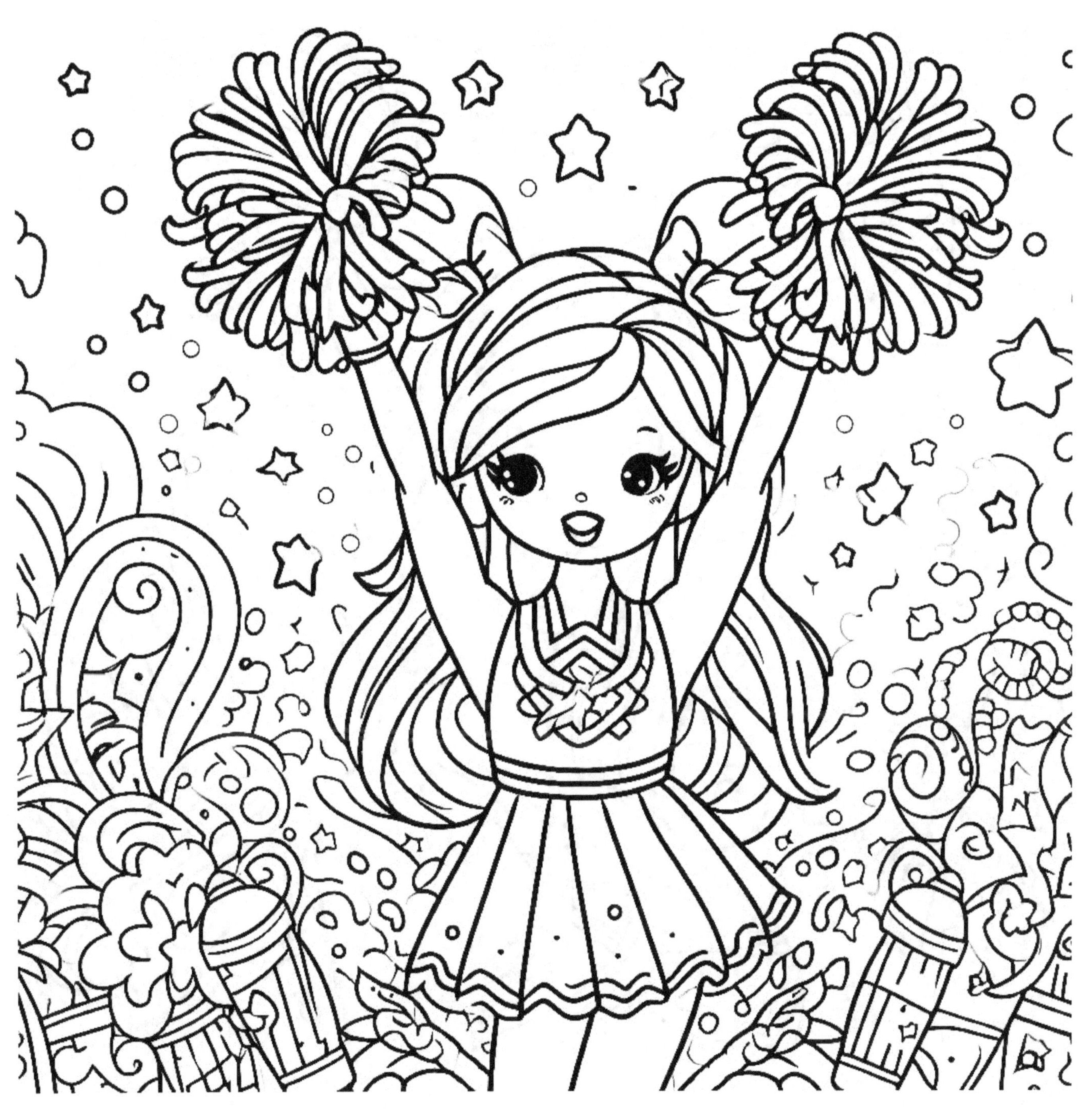

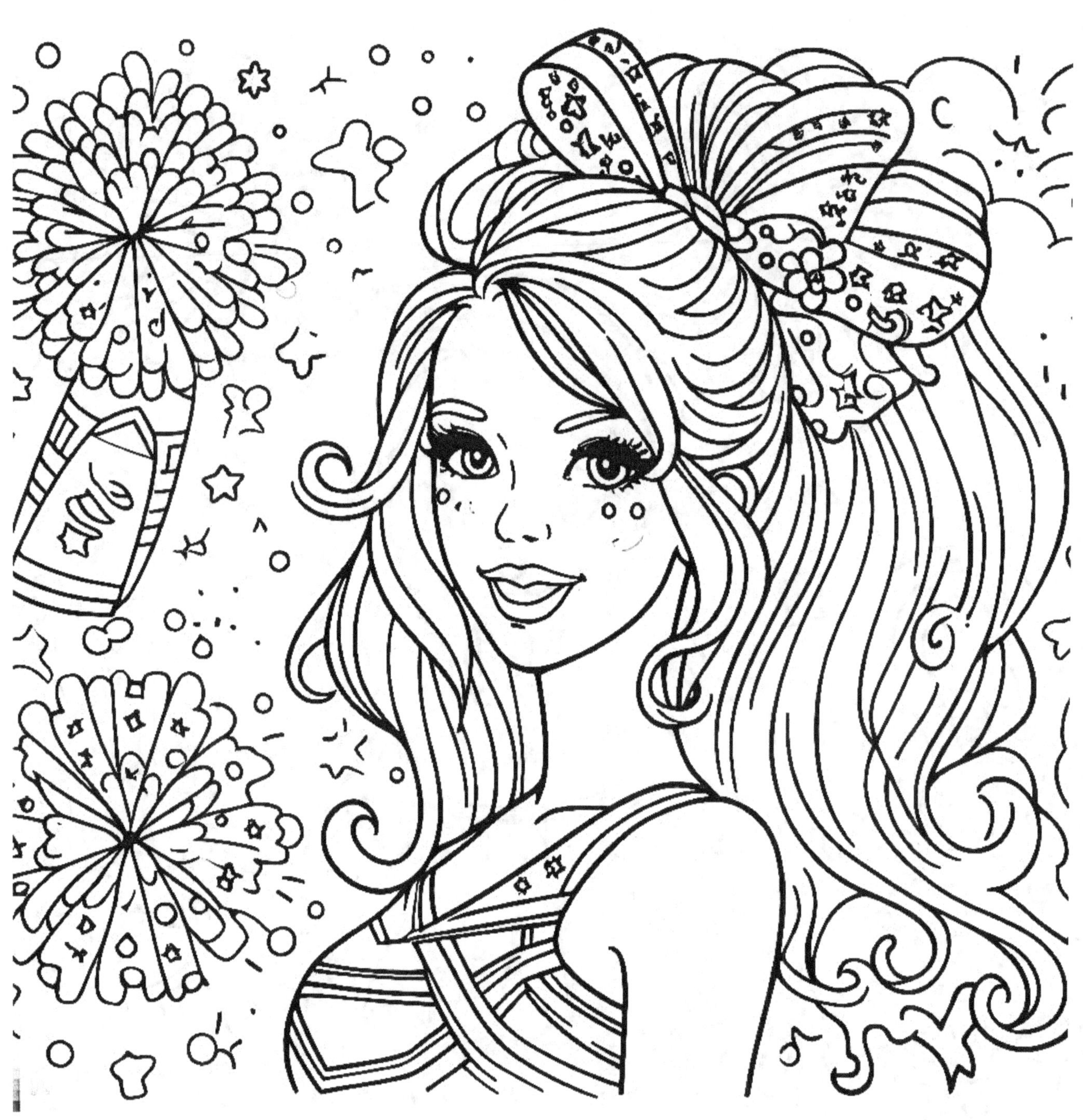

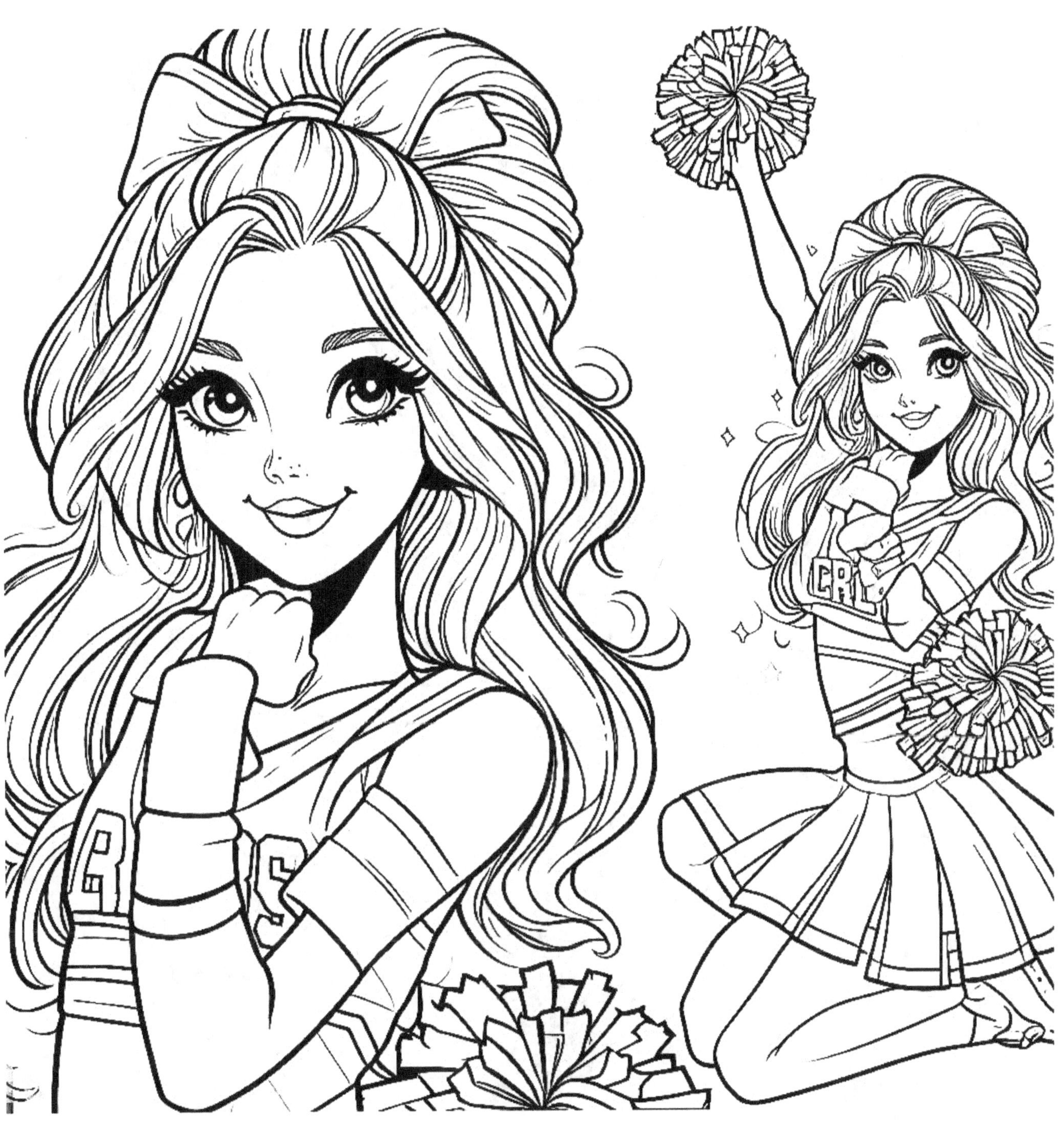

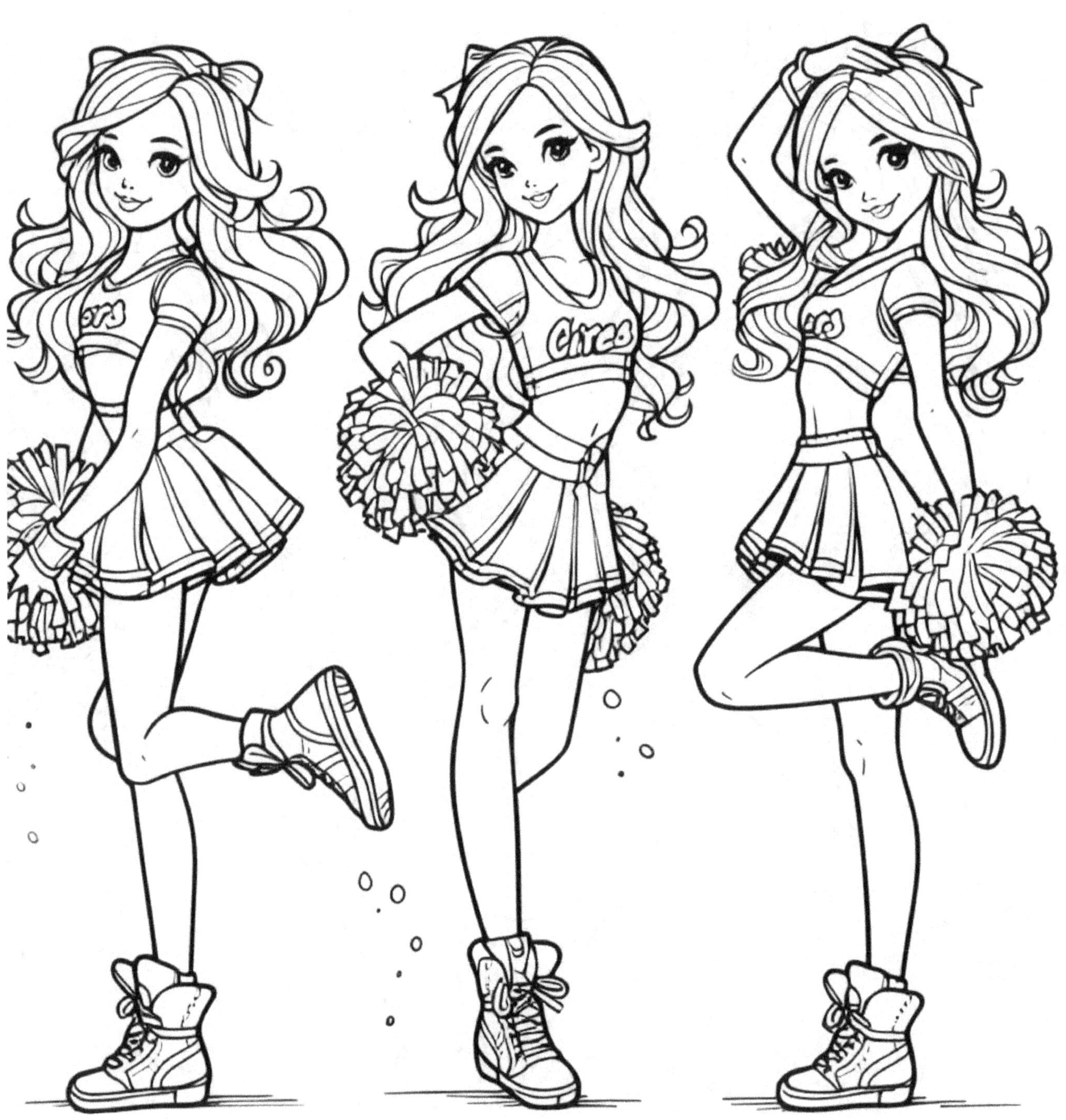

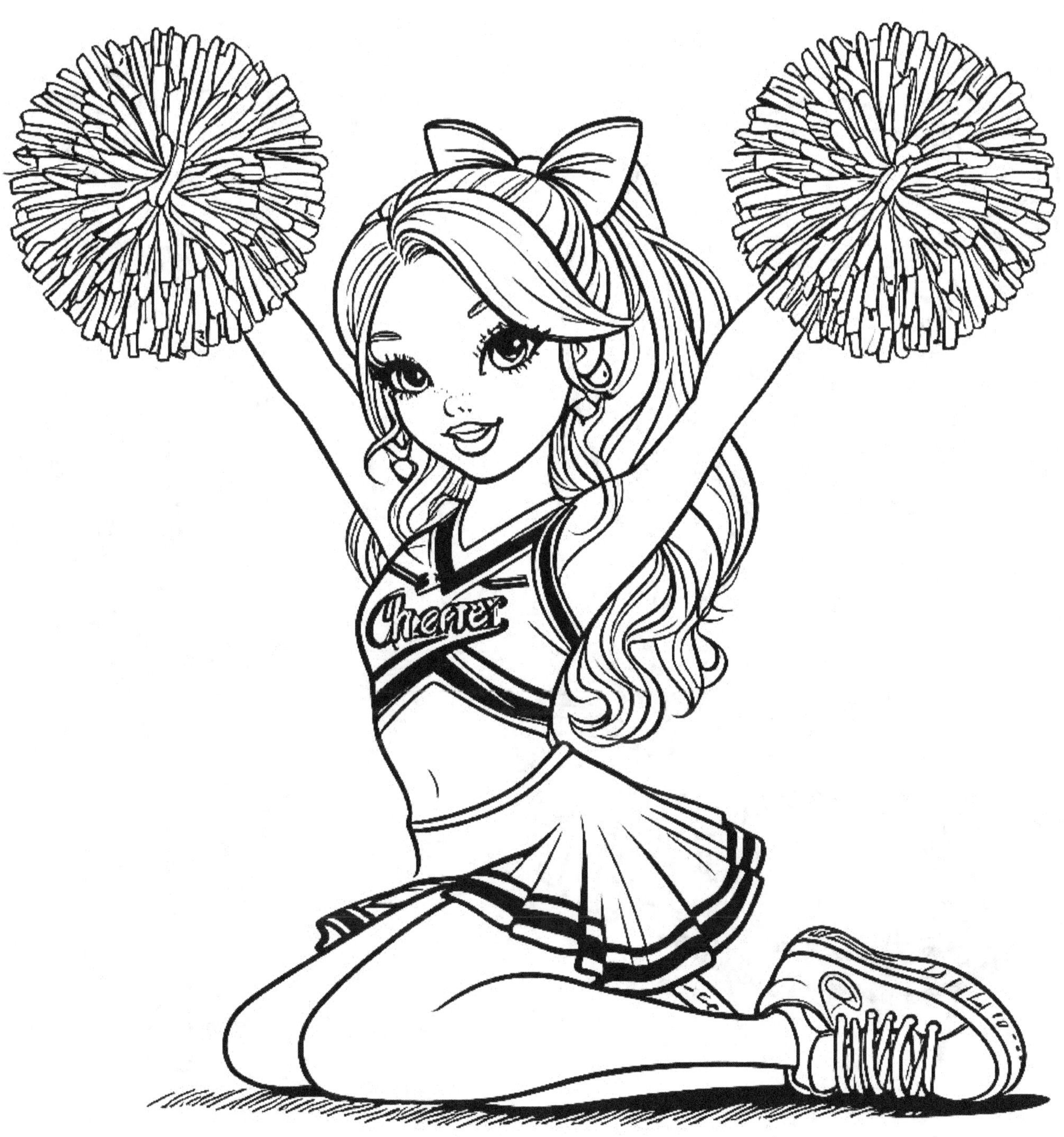

Cheer

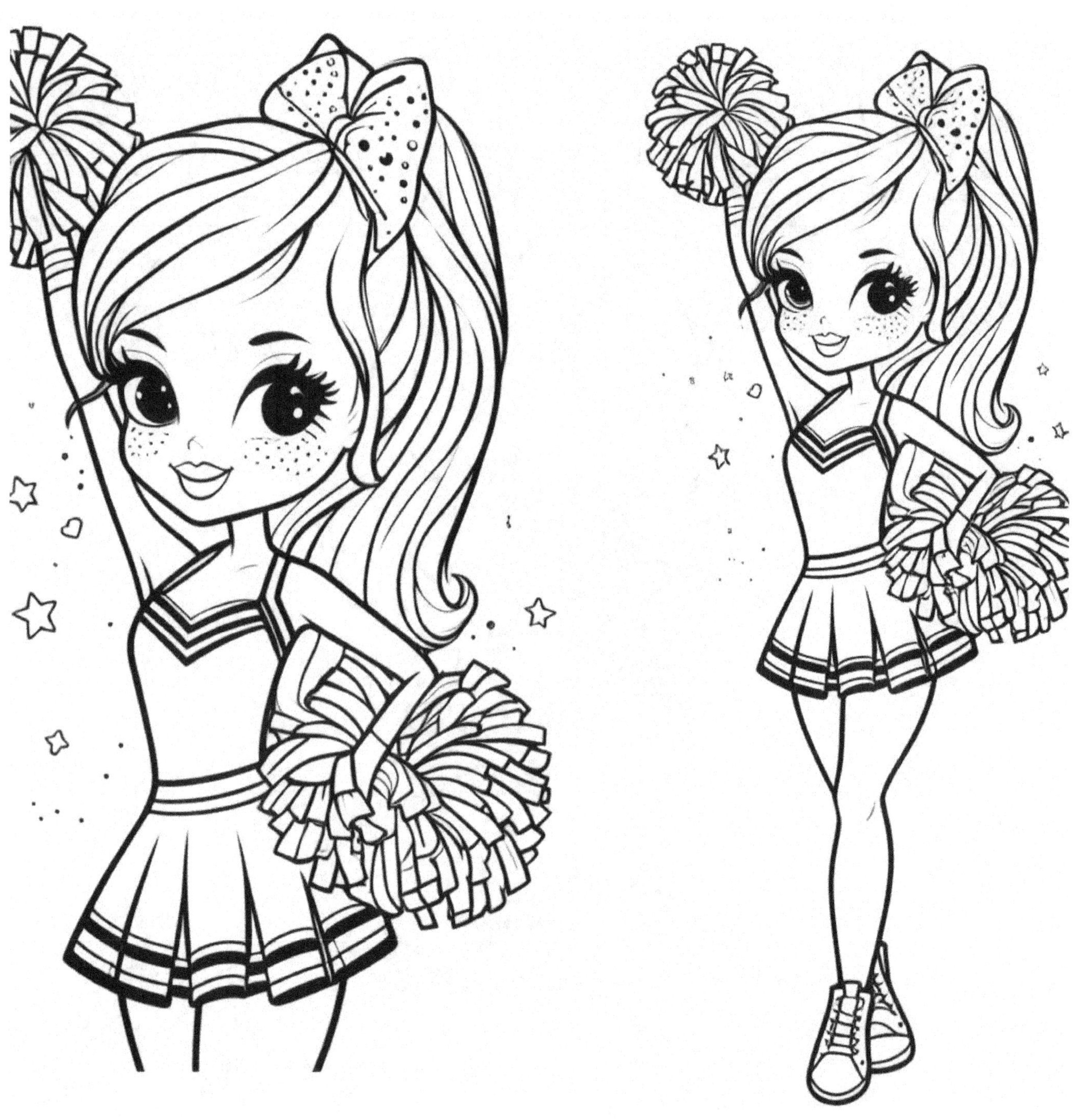

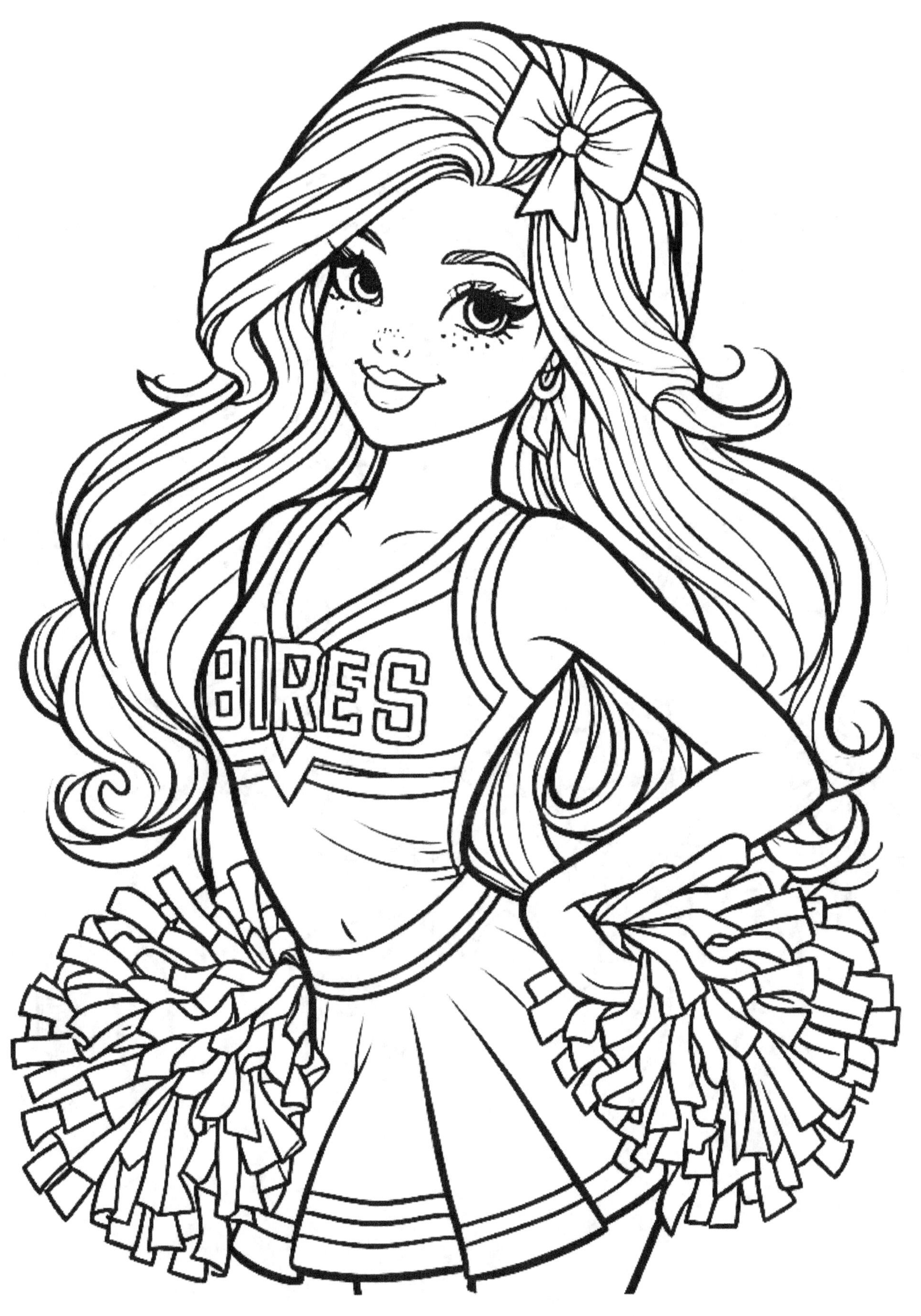

BIRES

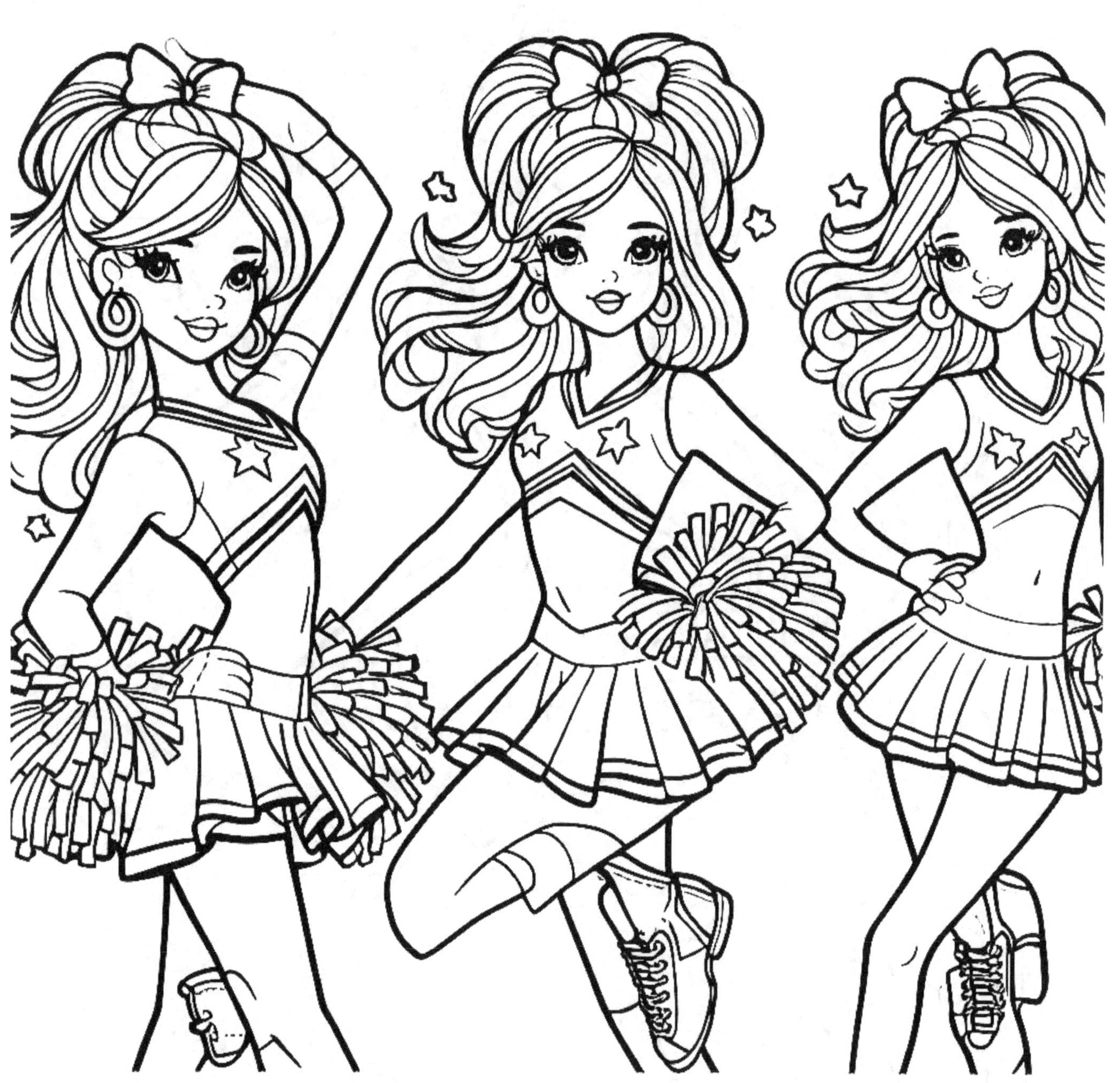

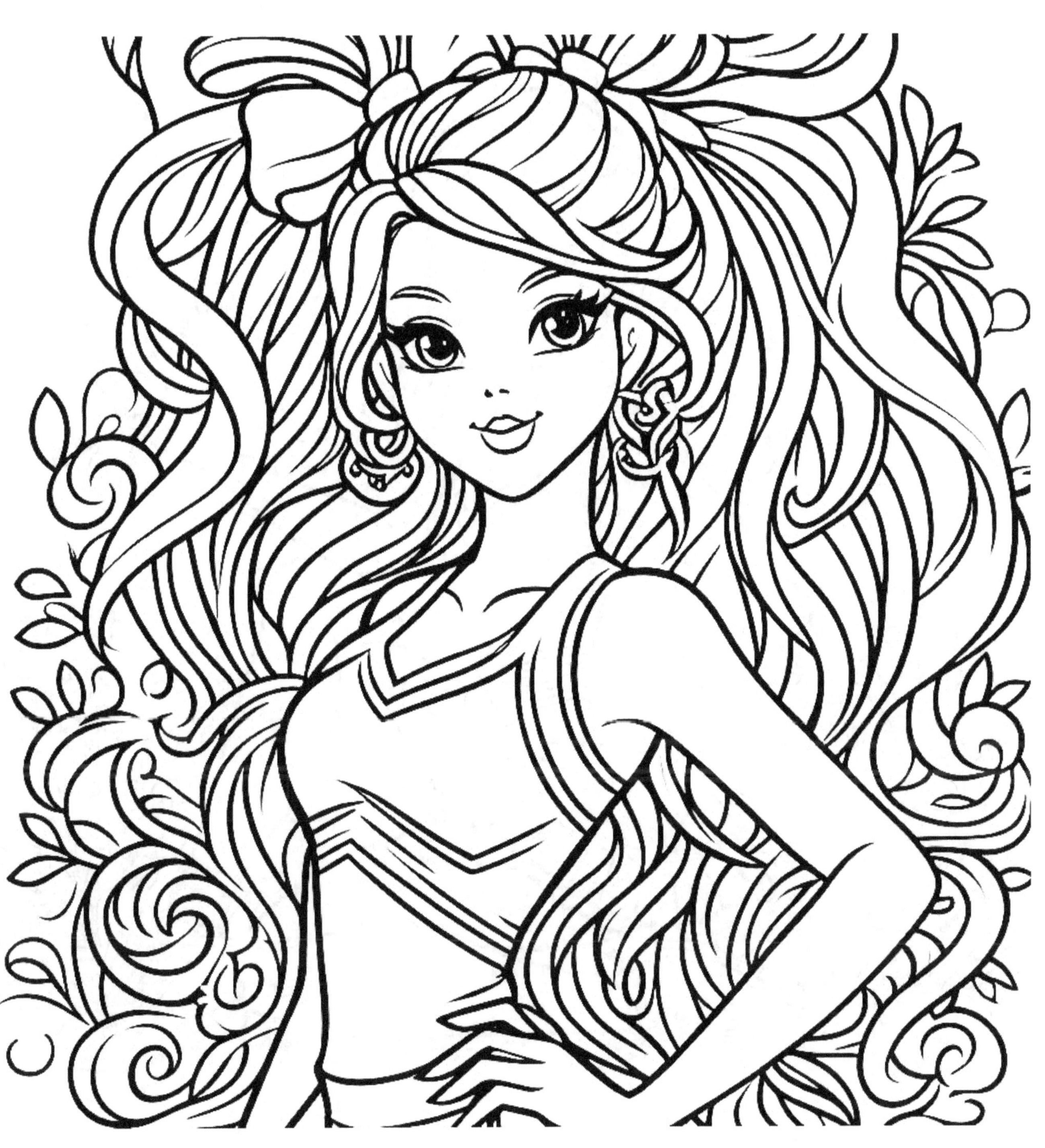

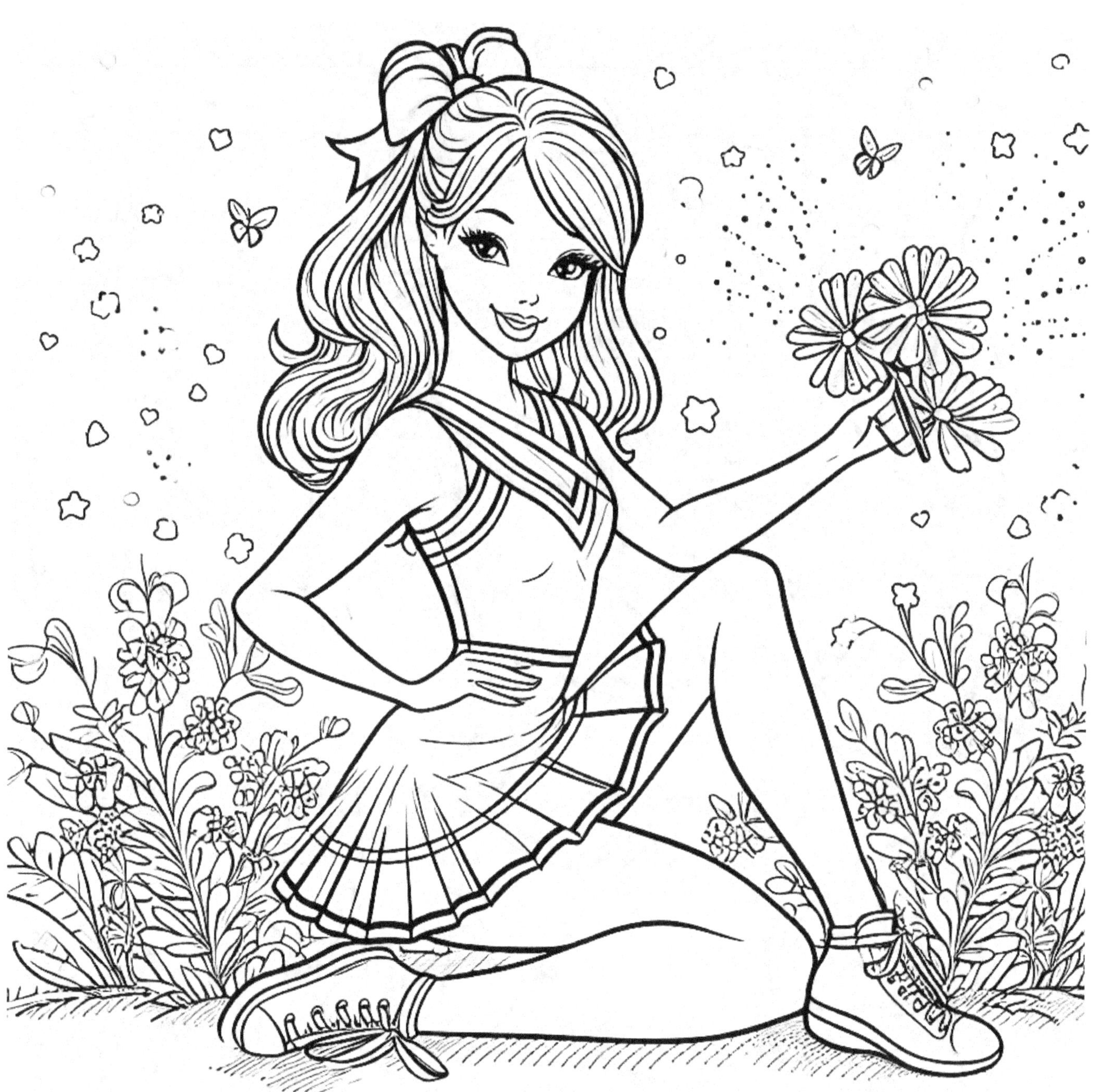

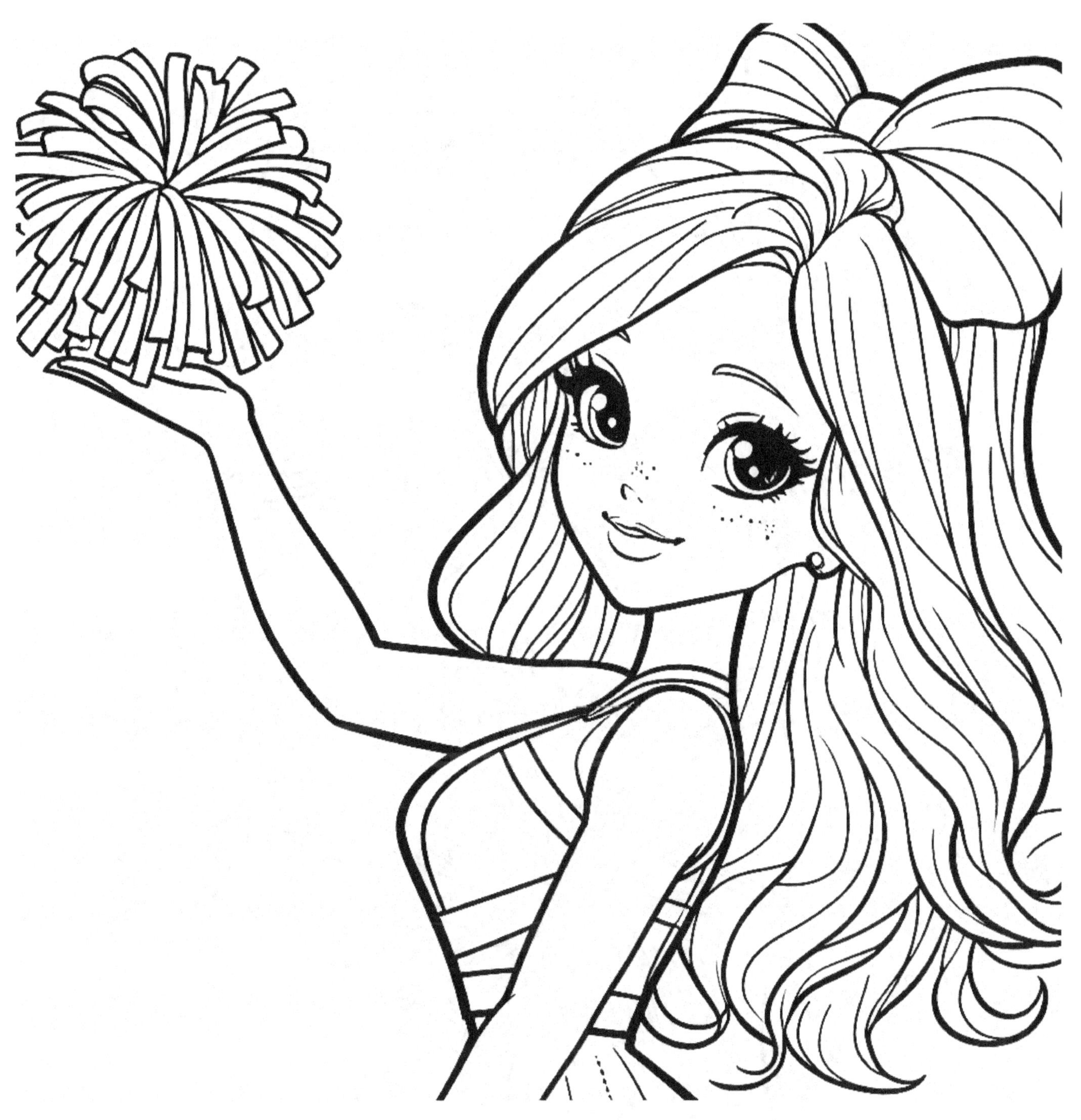

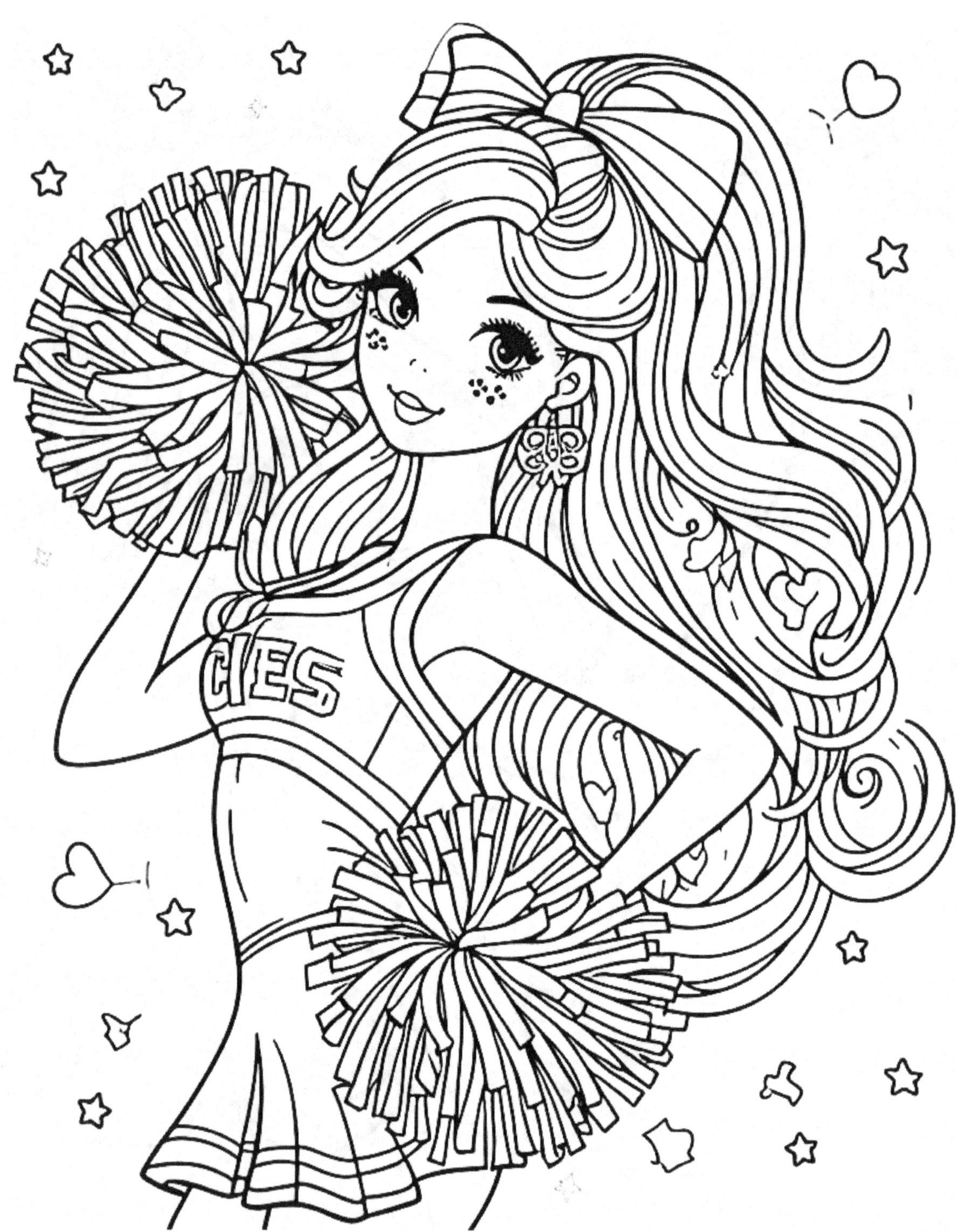

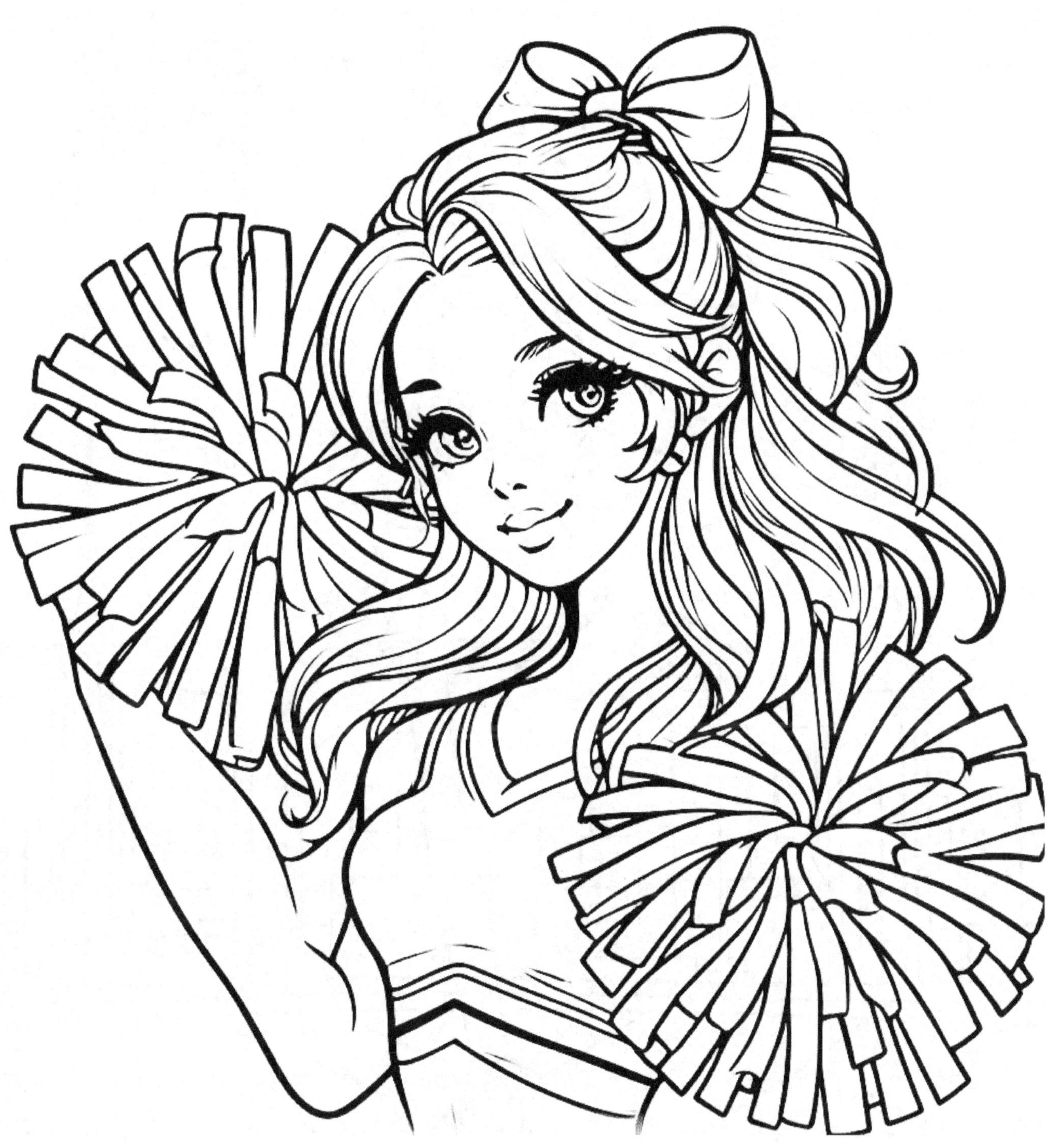

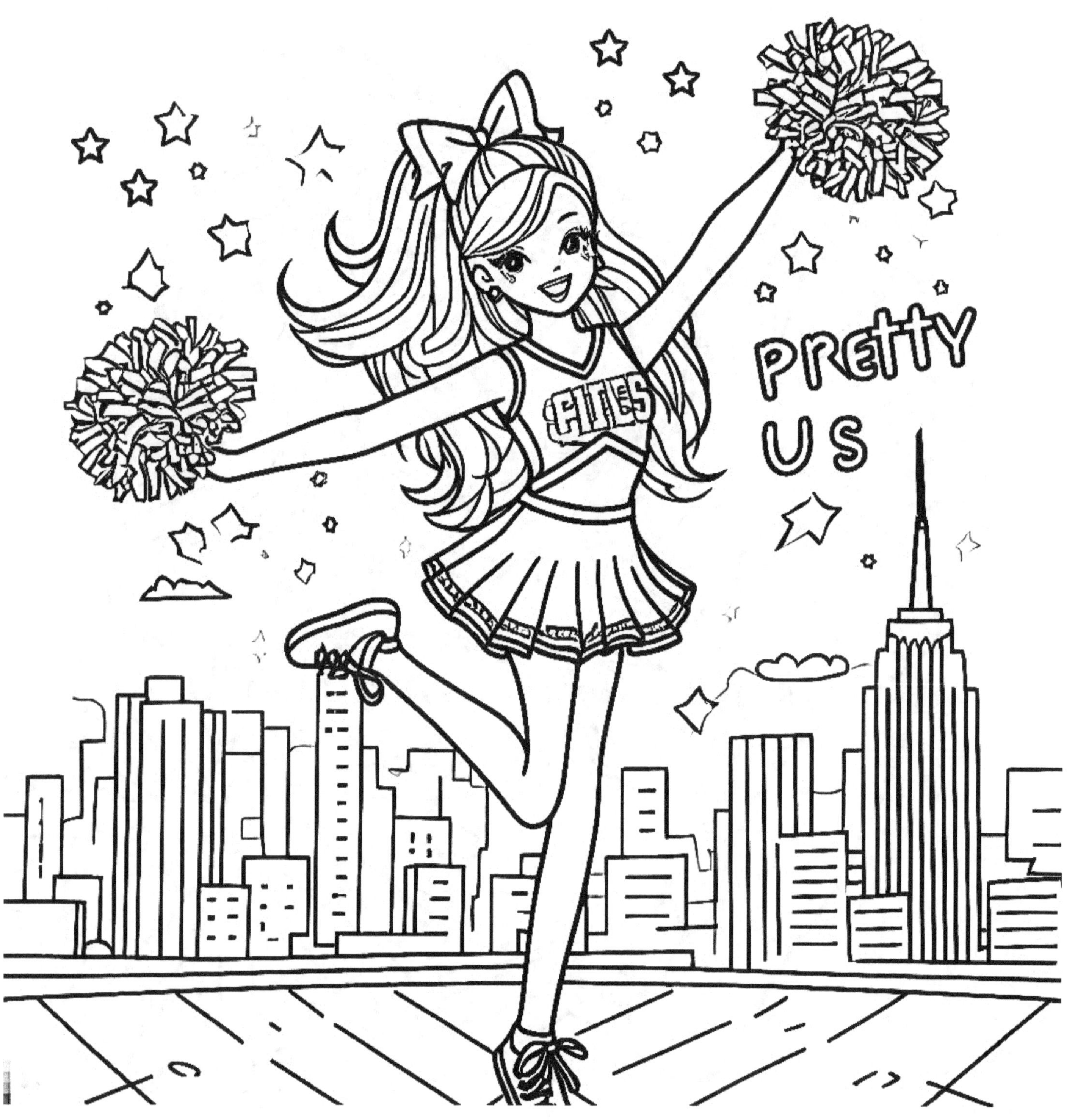

CITES
PRETTY
US

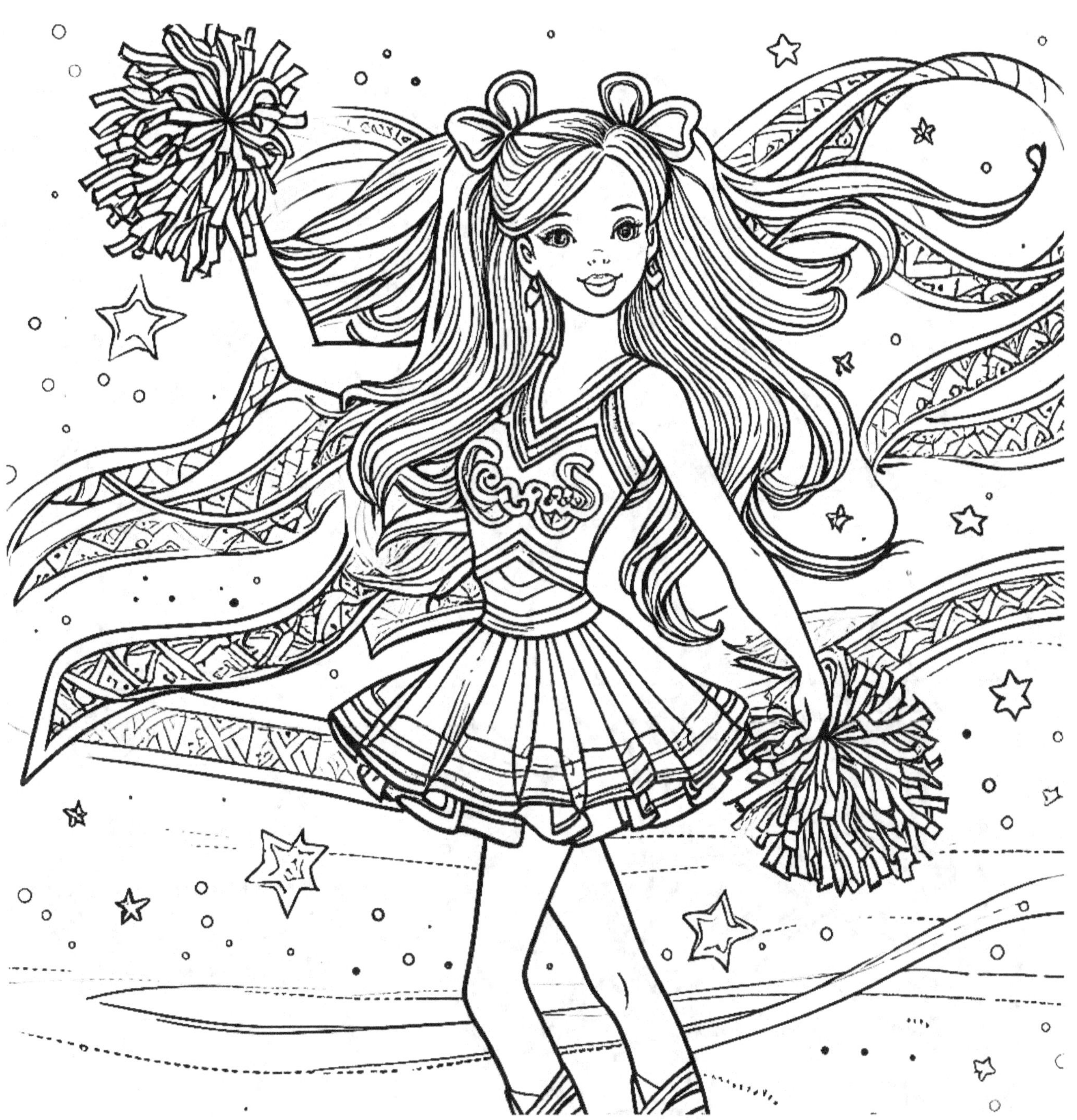

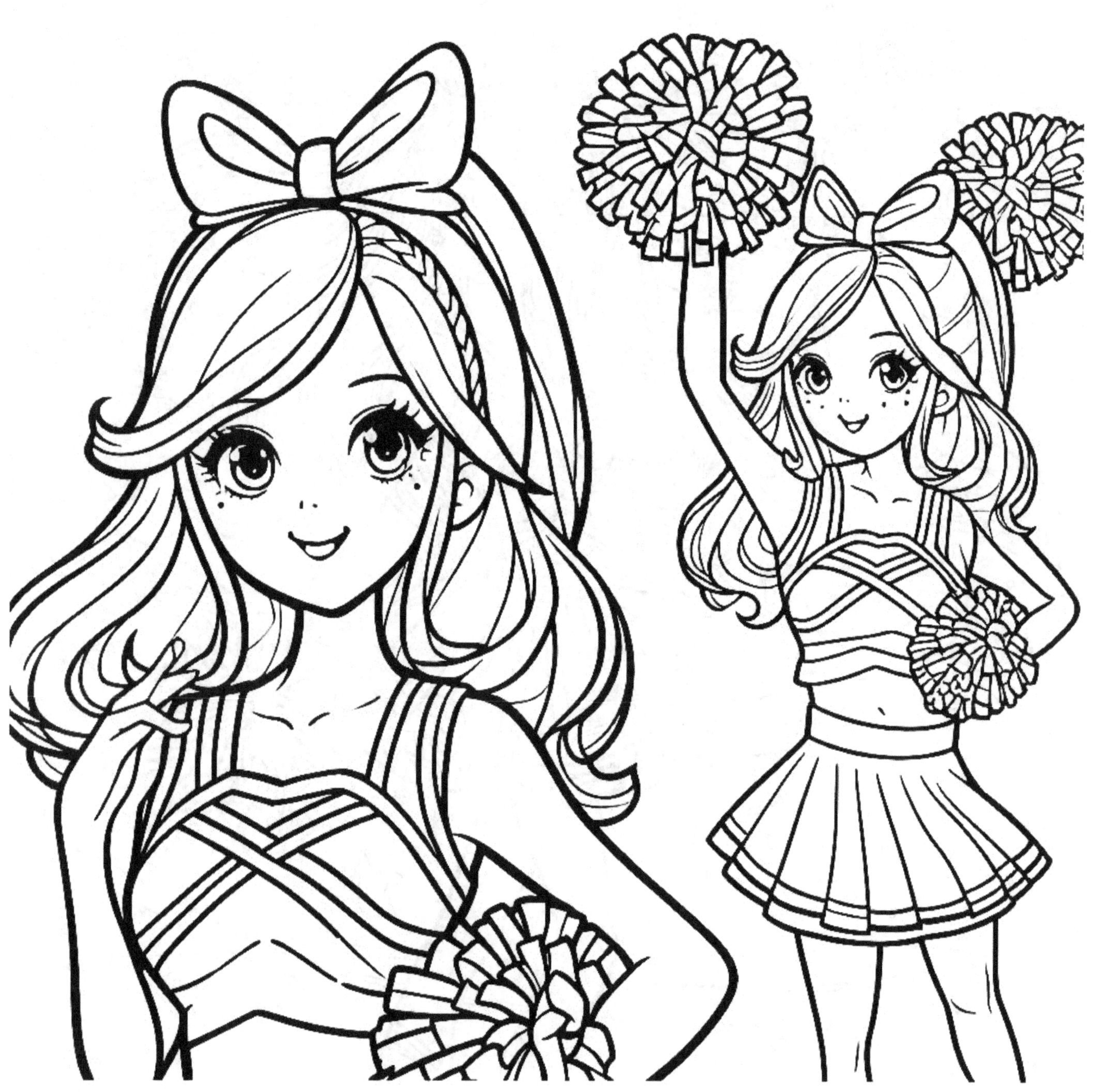

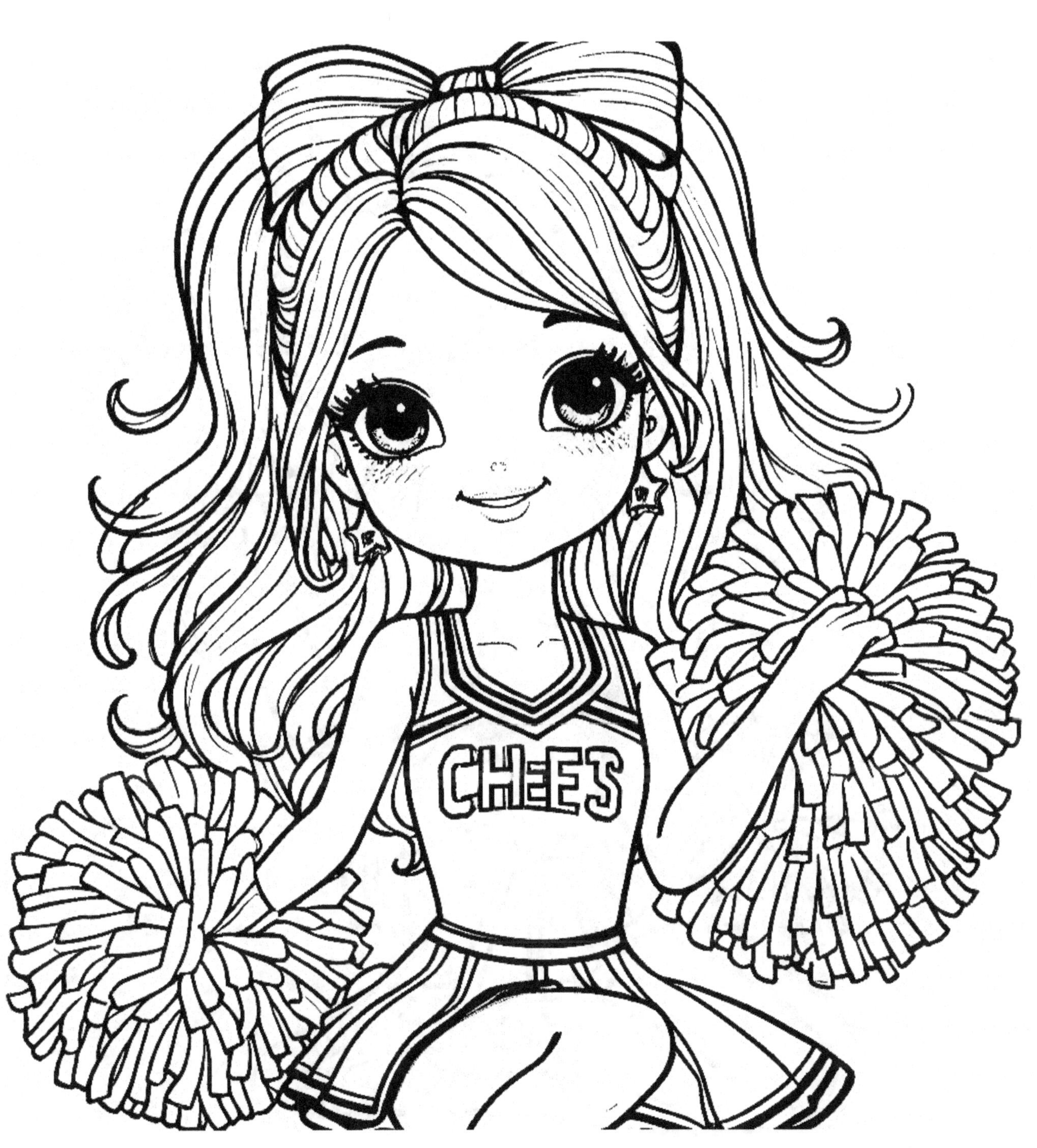
CHEES

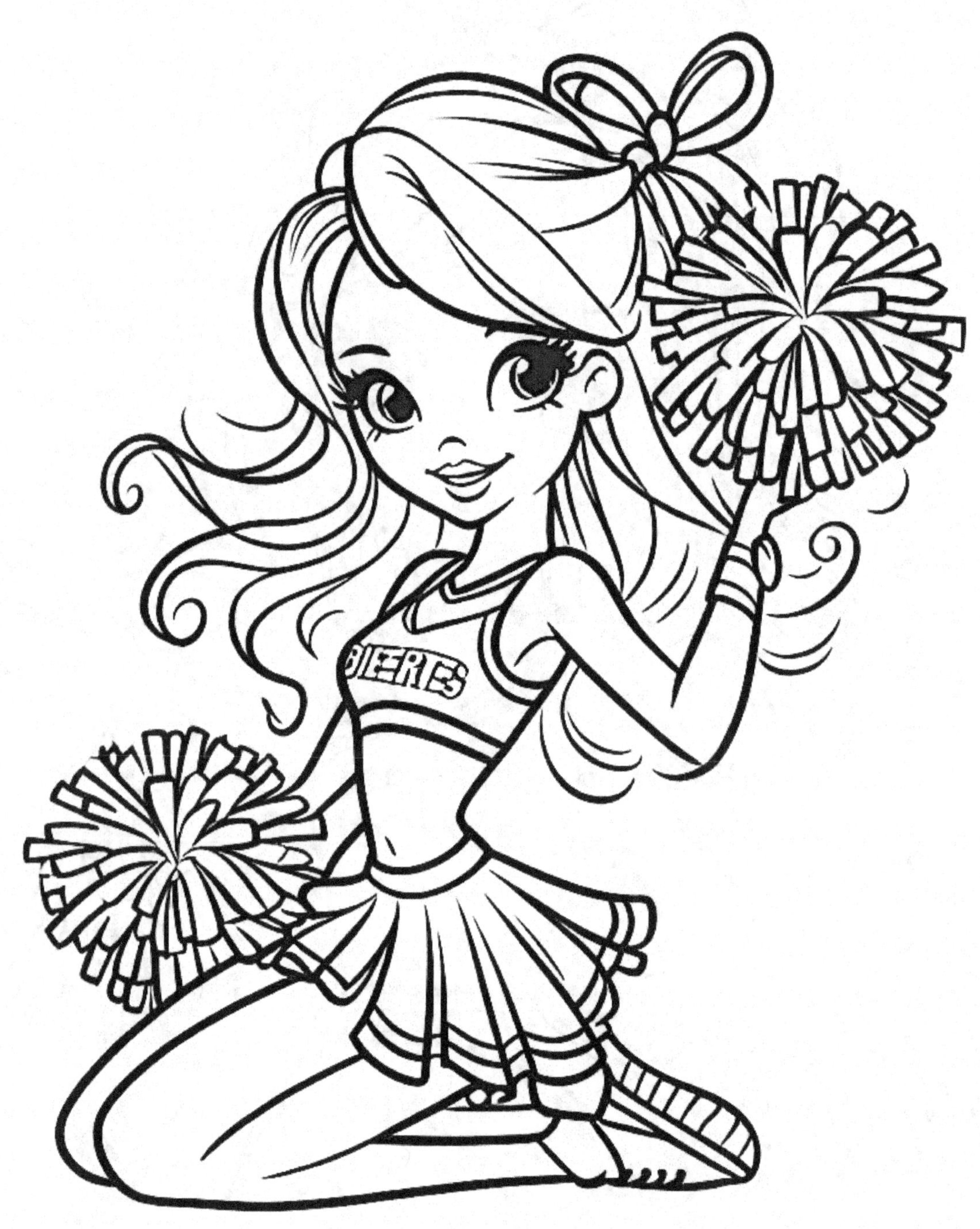
BIERES

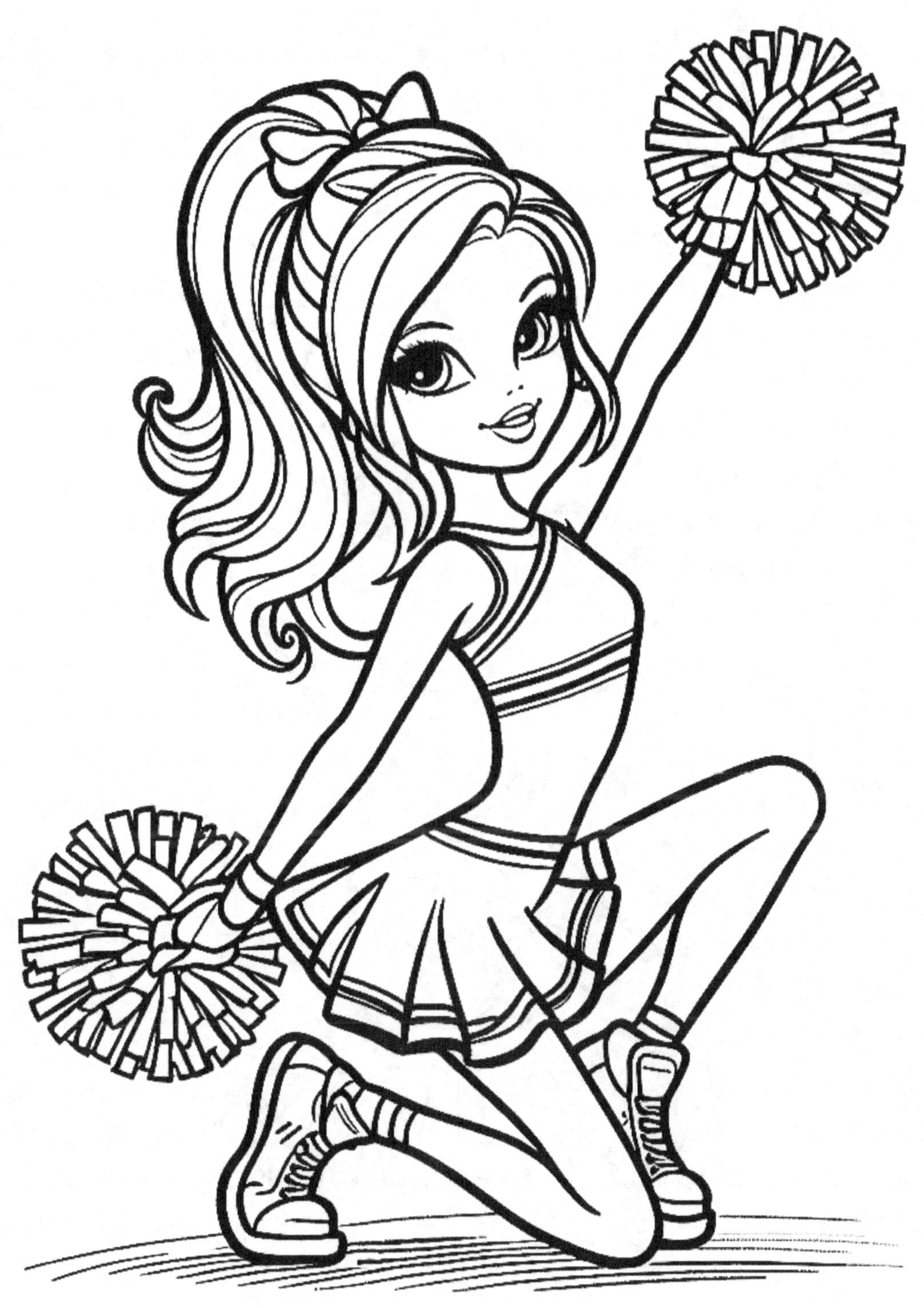

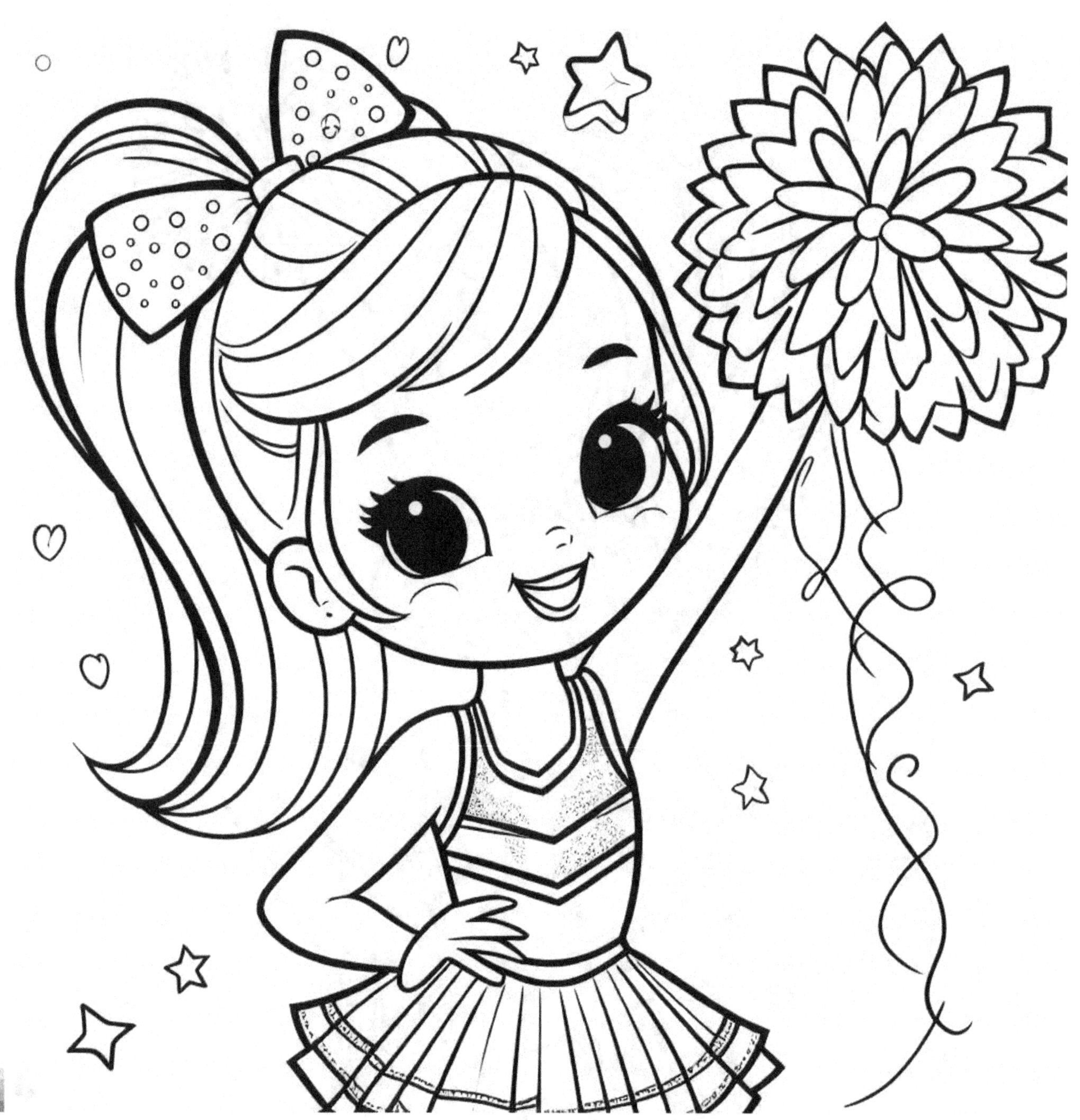

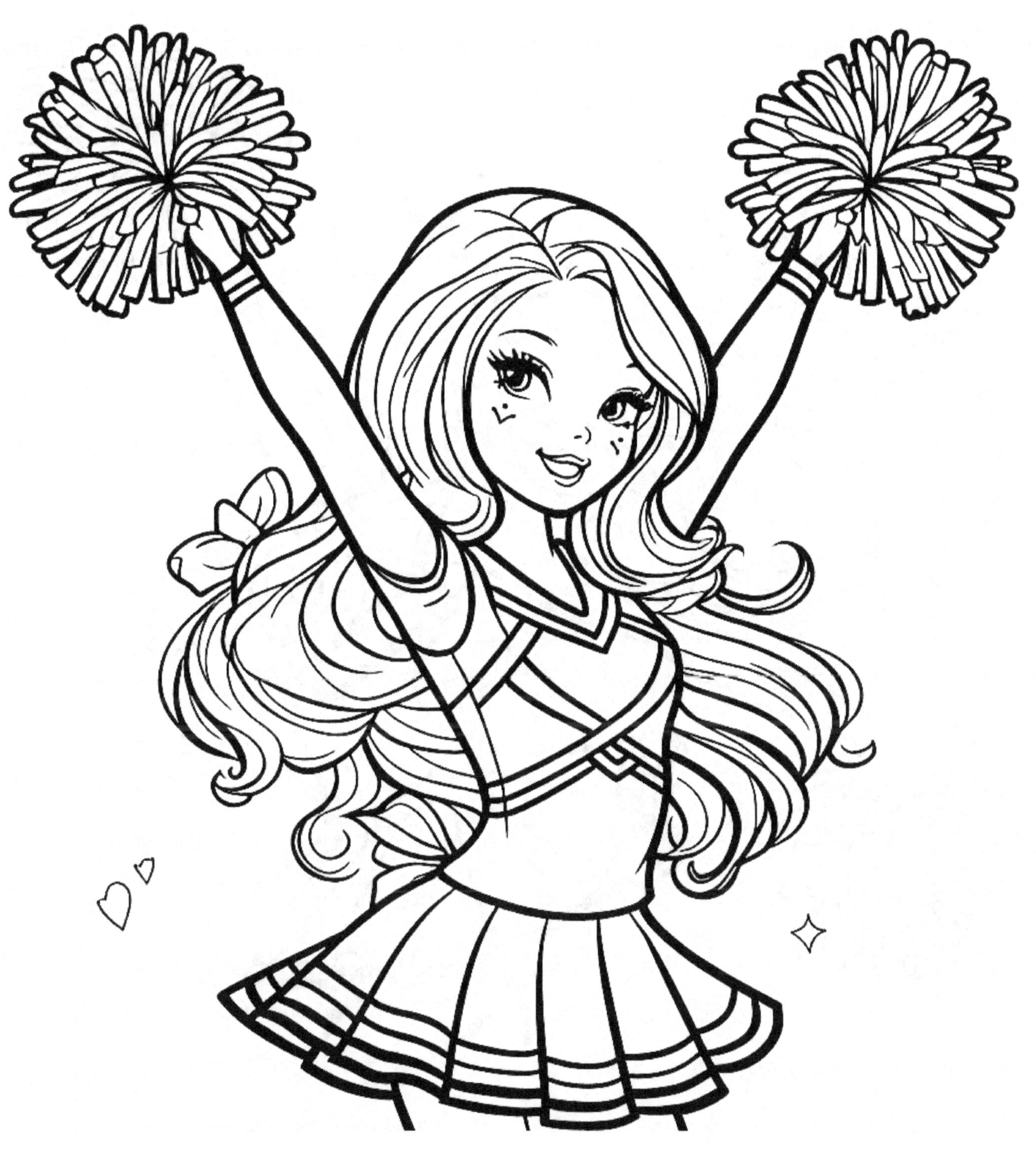

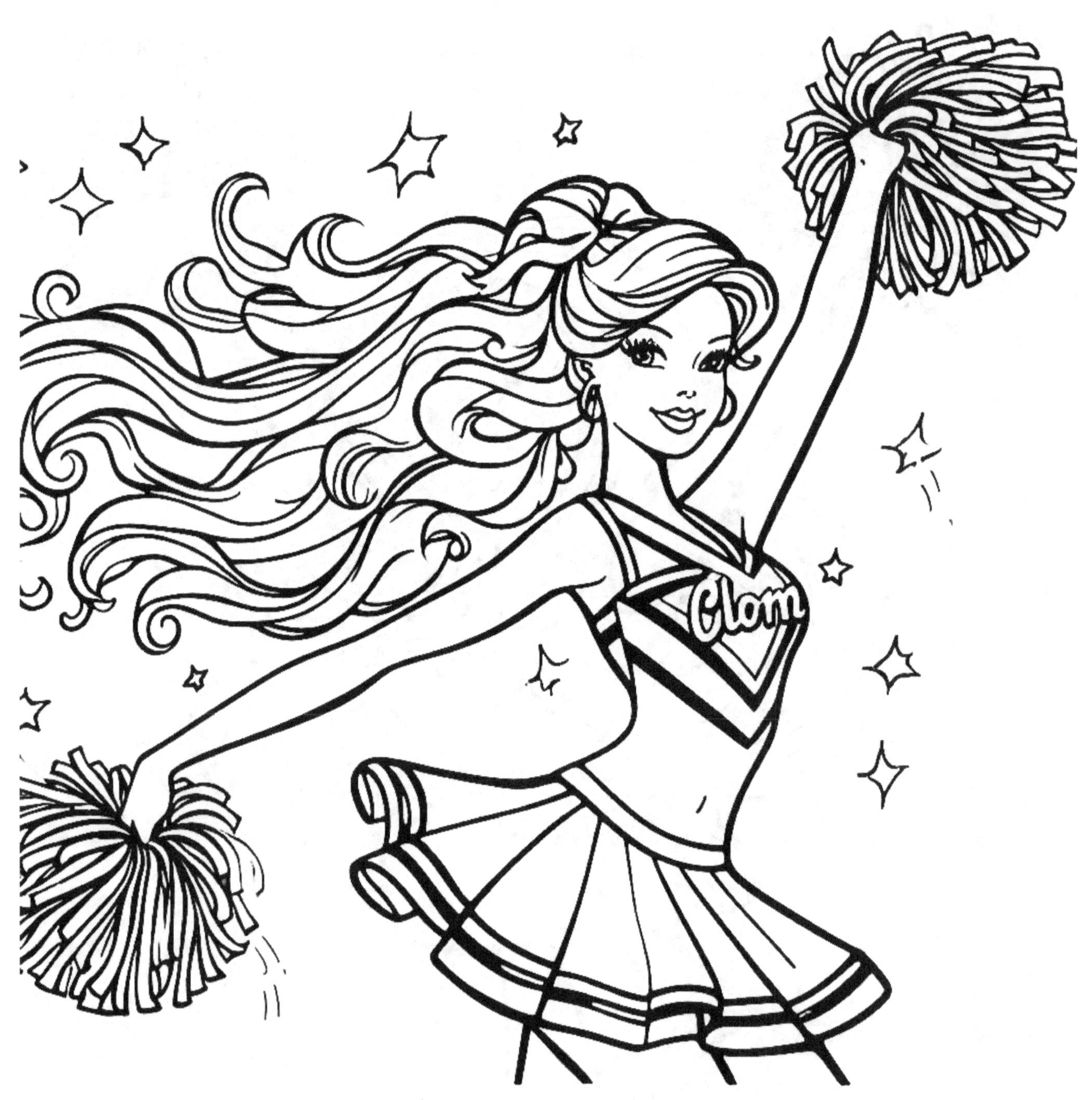
Glam

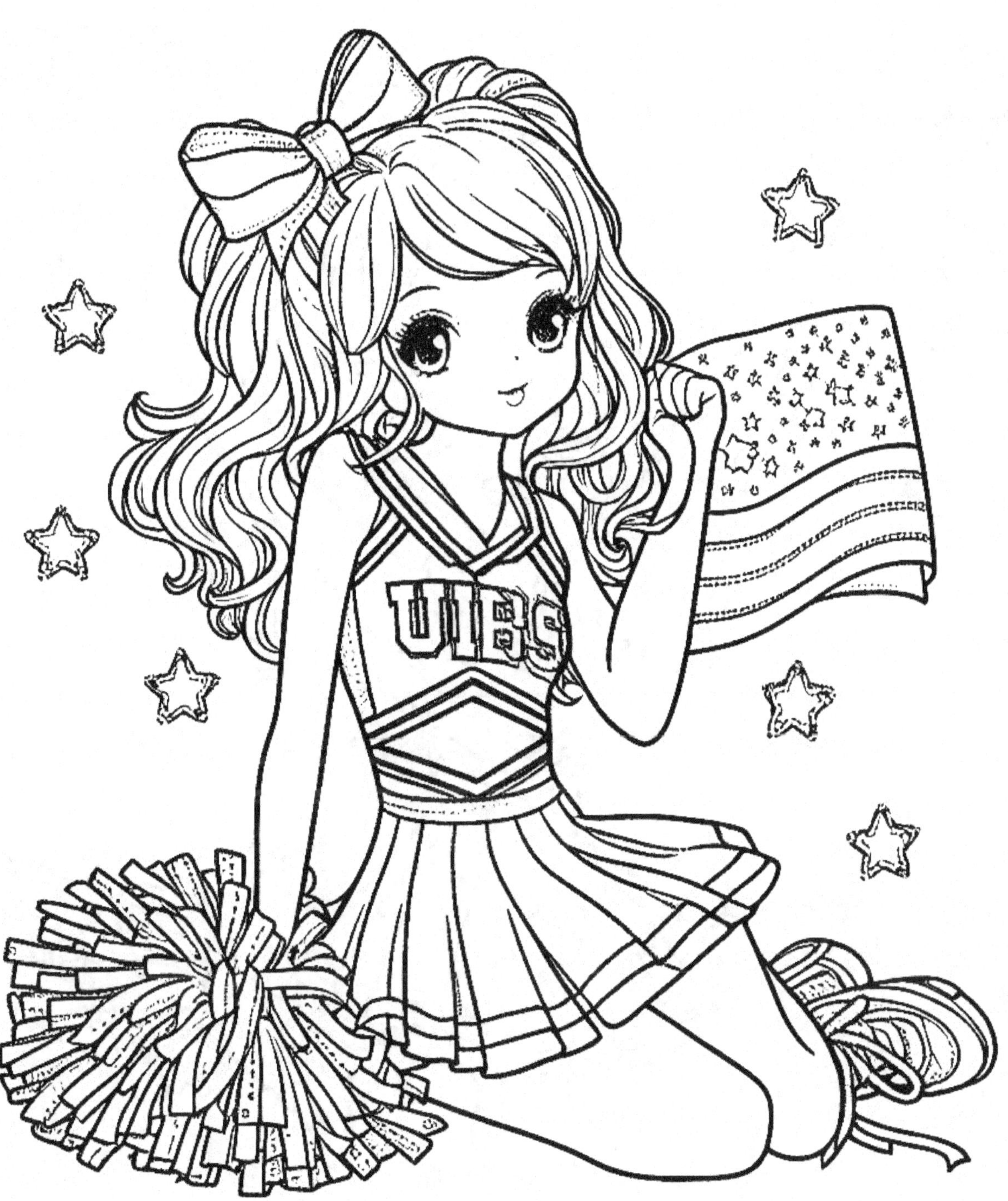

UIBS

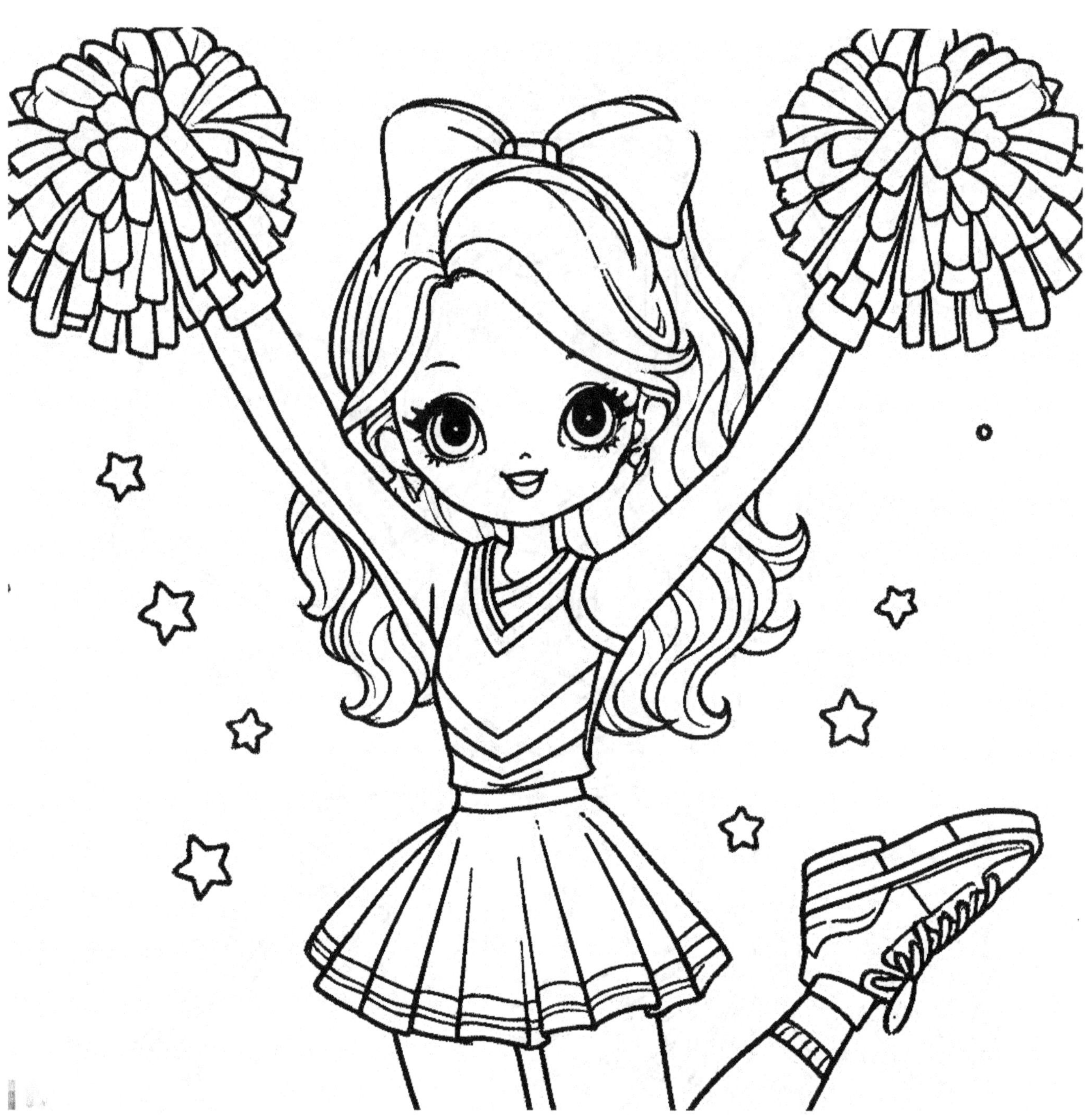

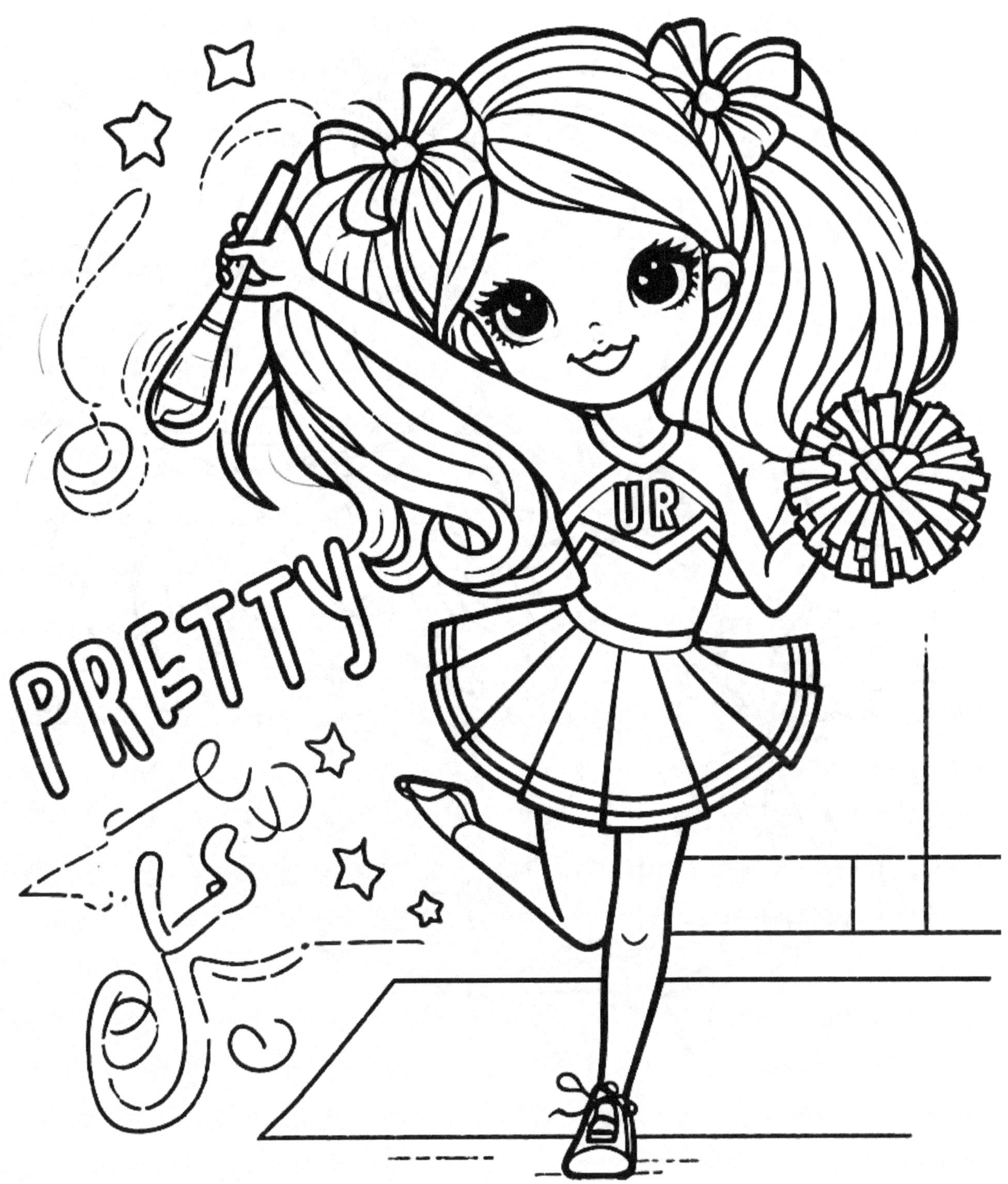

PRETTY
UR

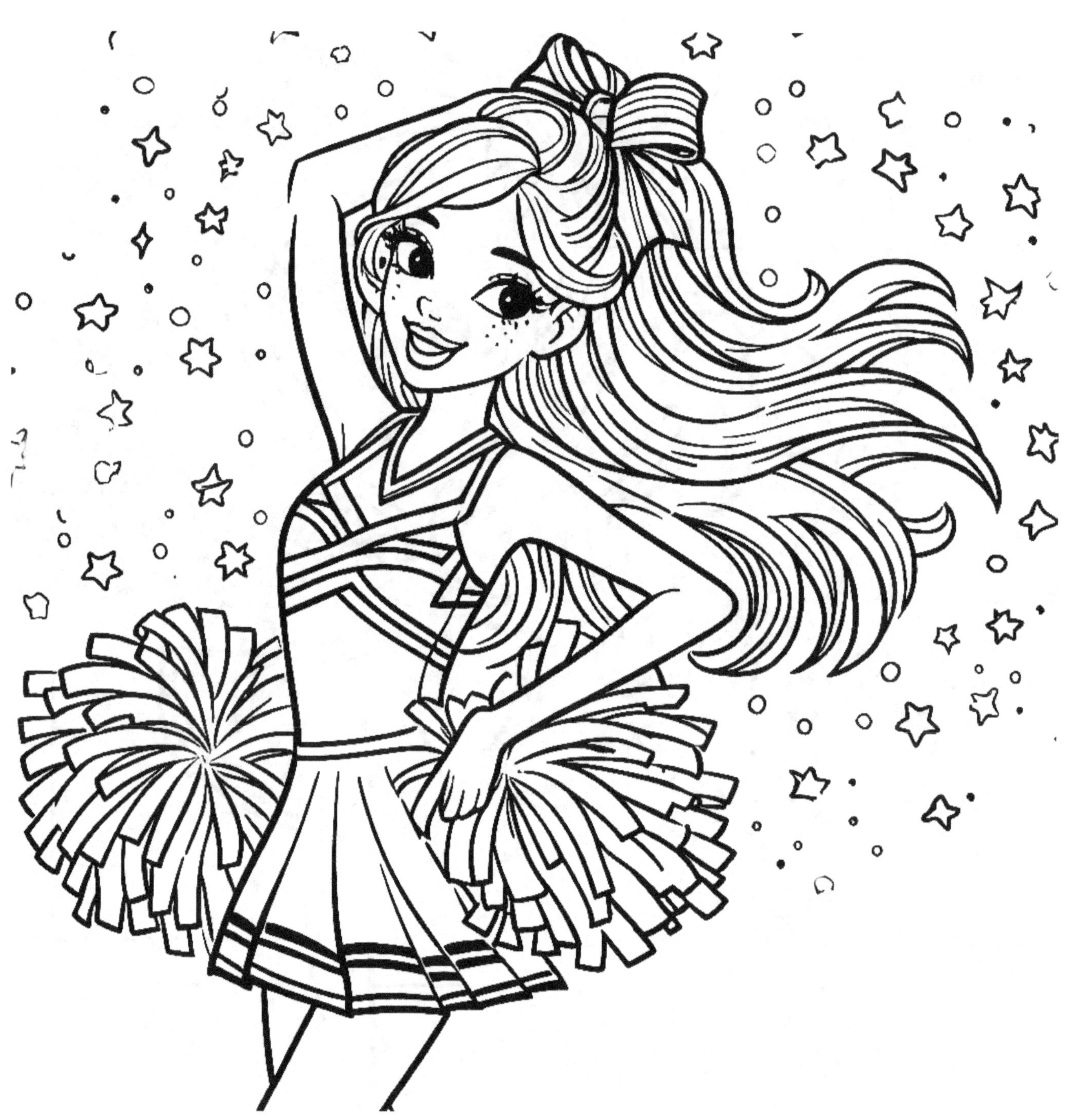

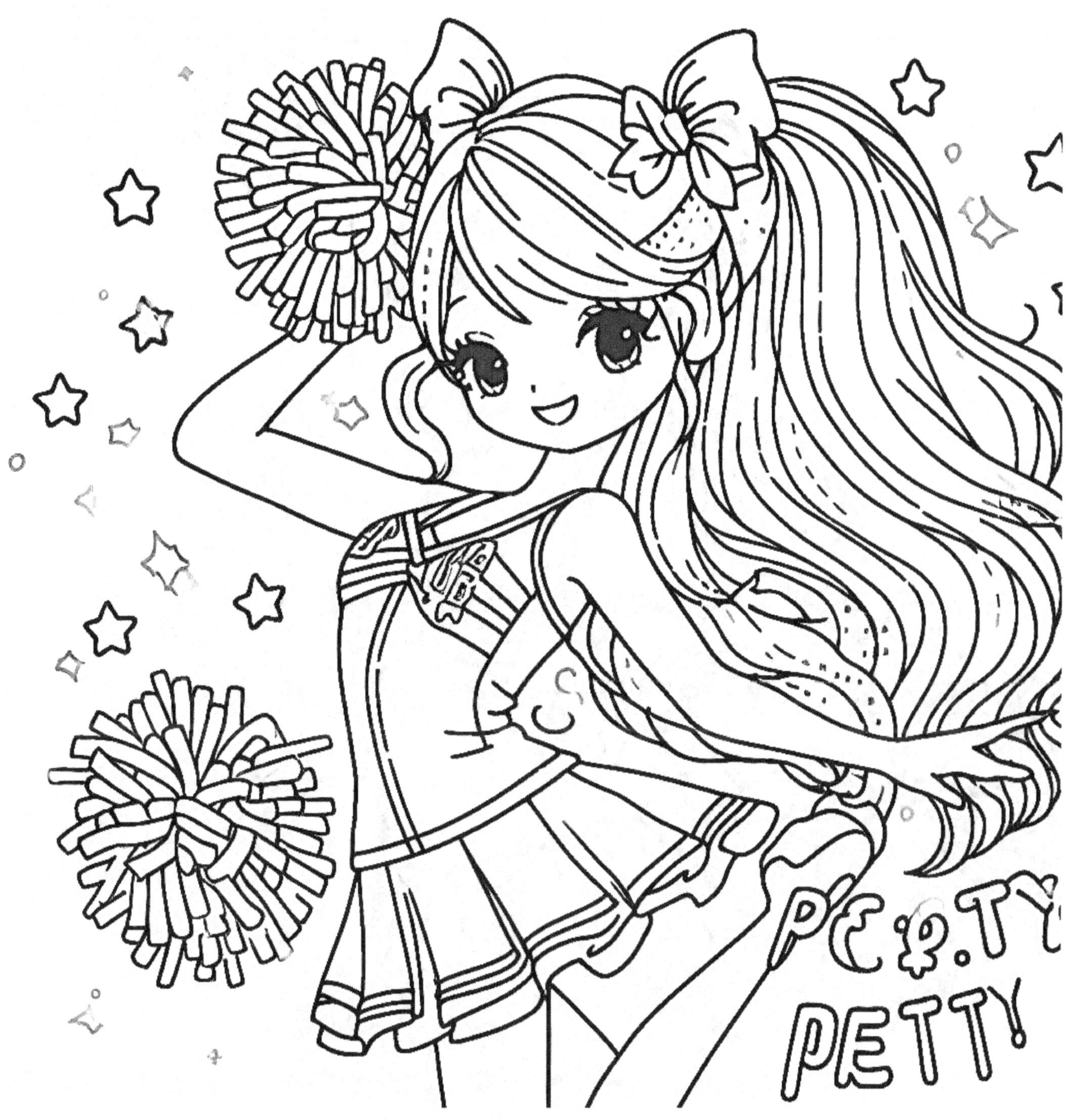

PRETTY
PETTY!

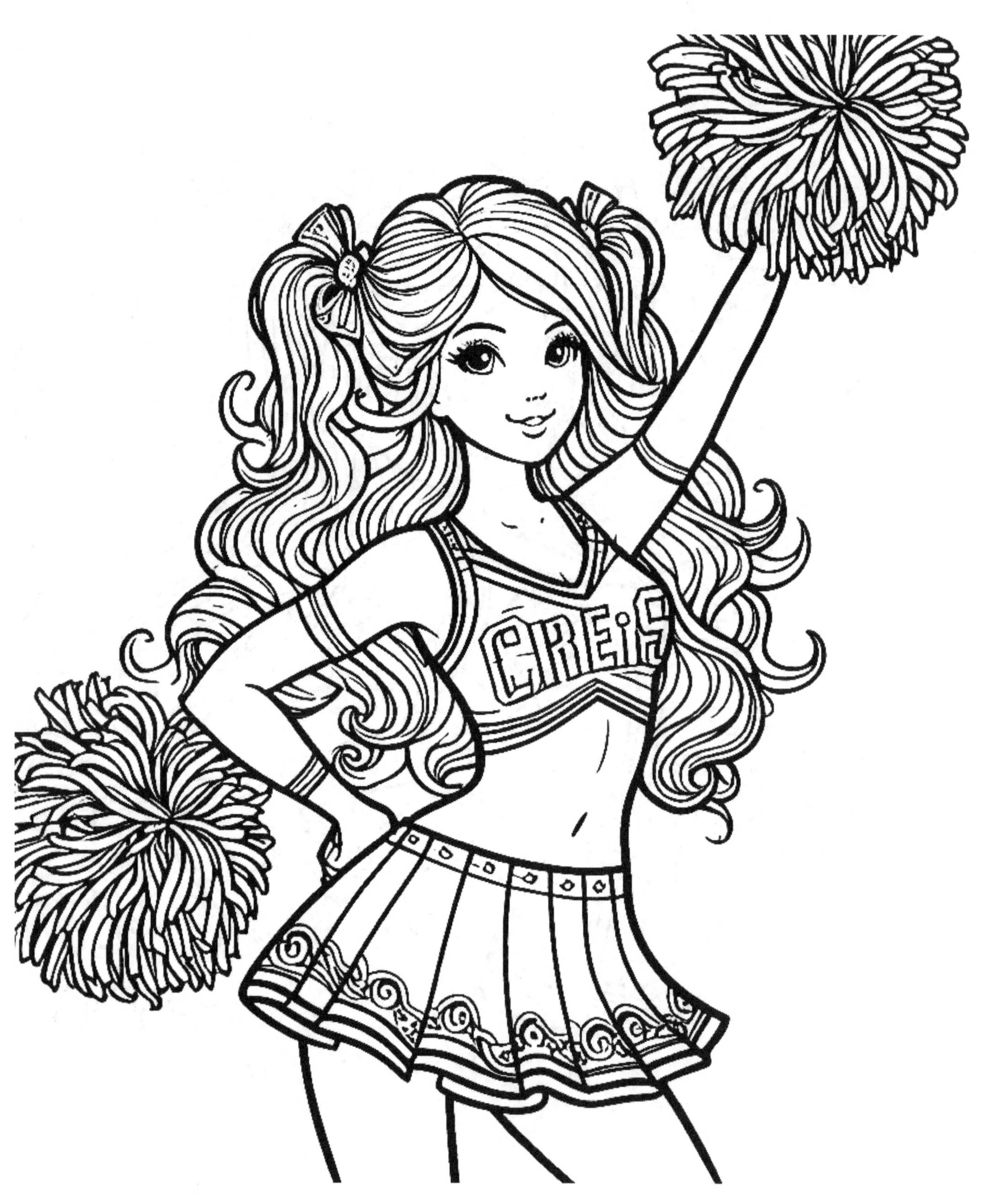

CREIS

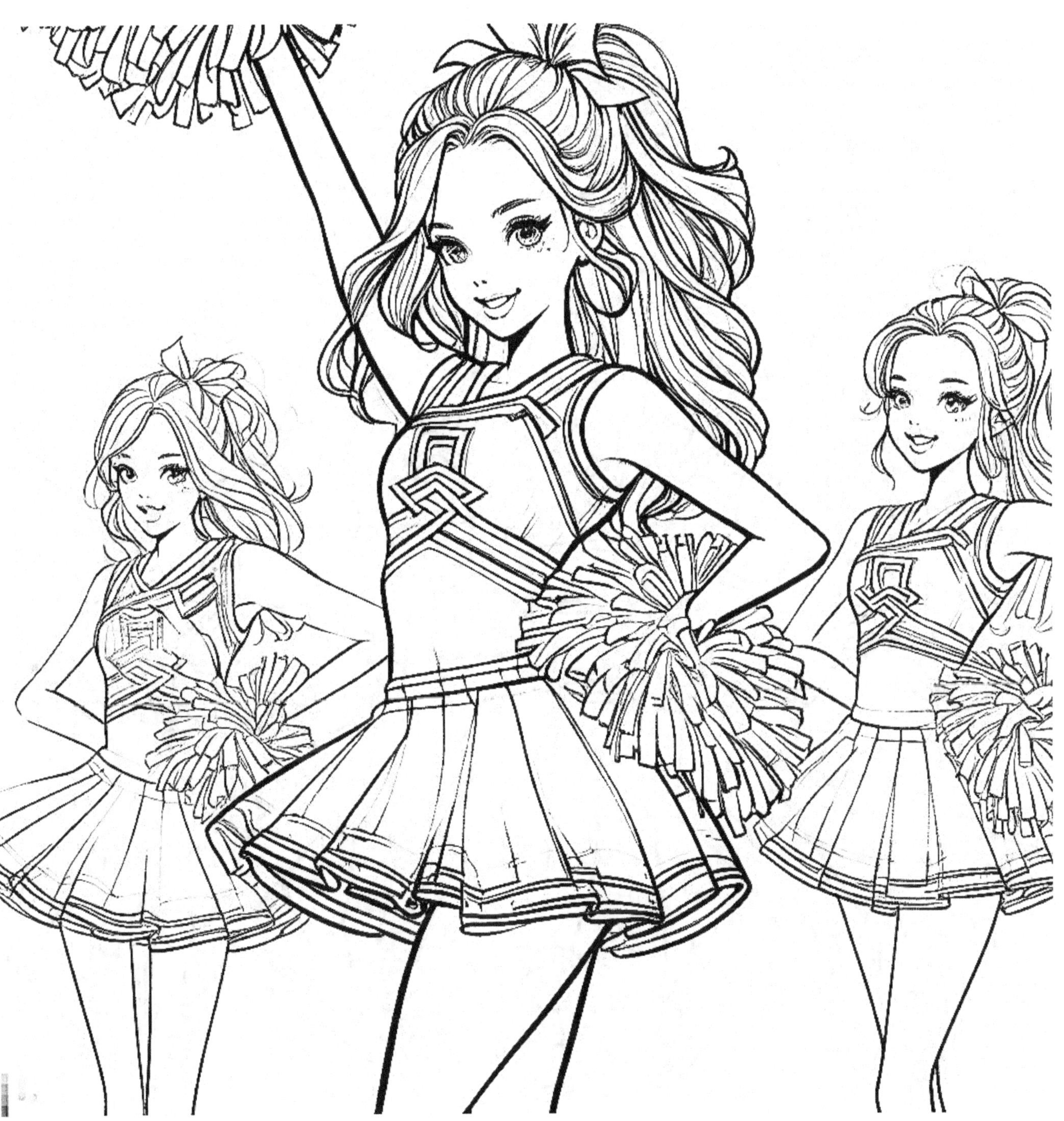

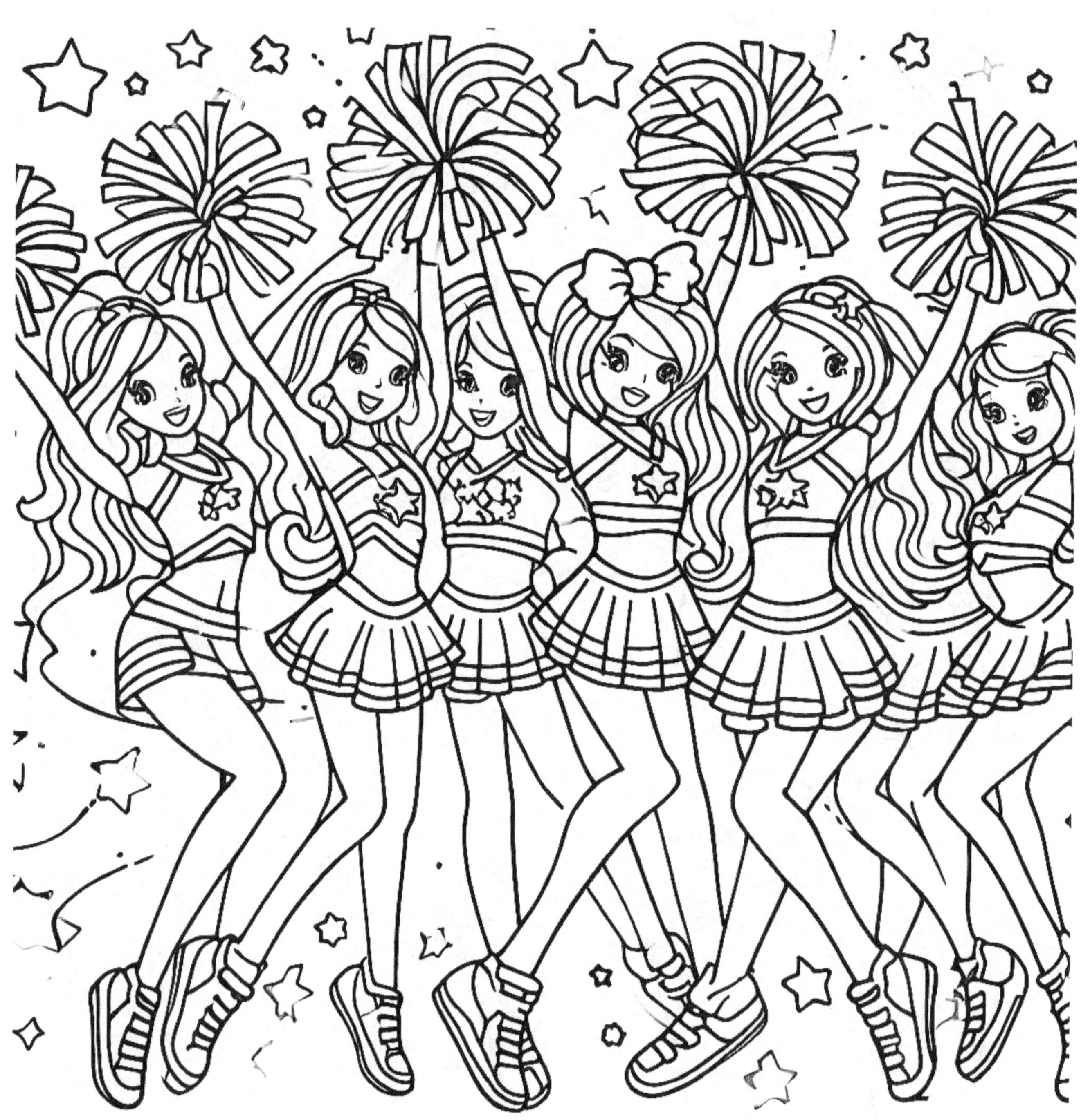

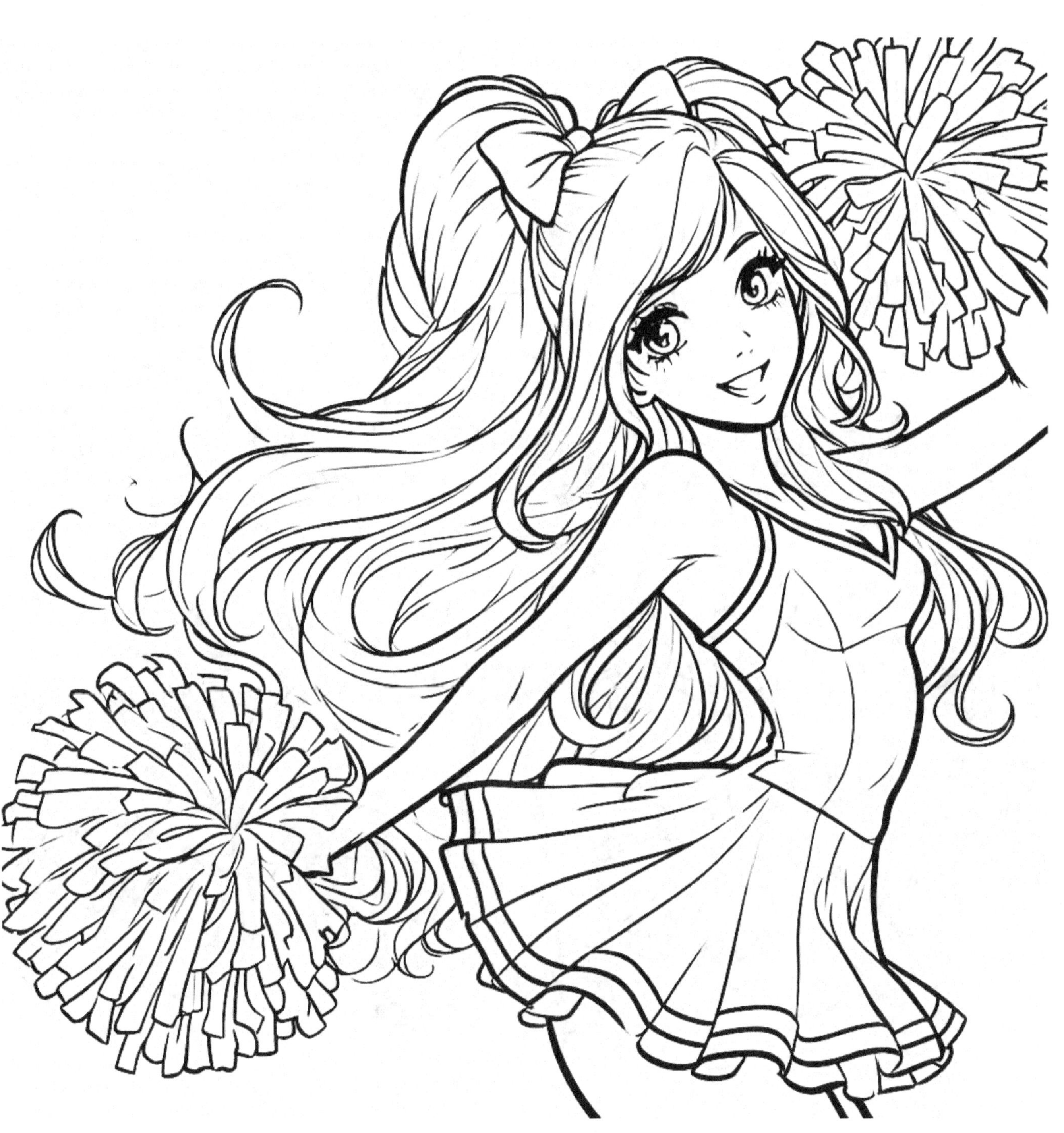

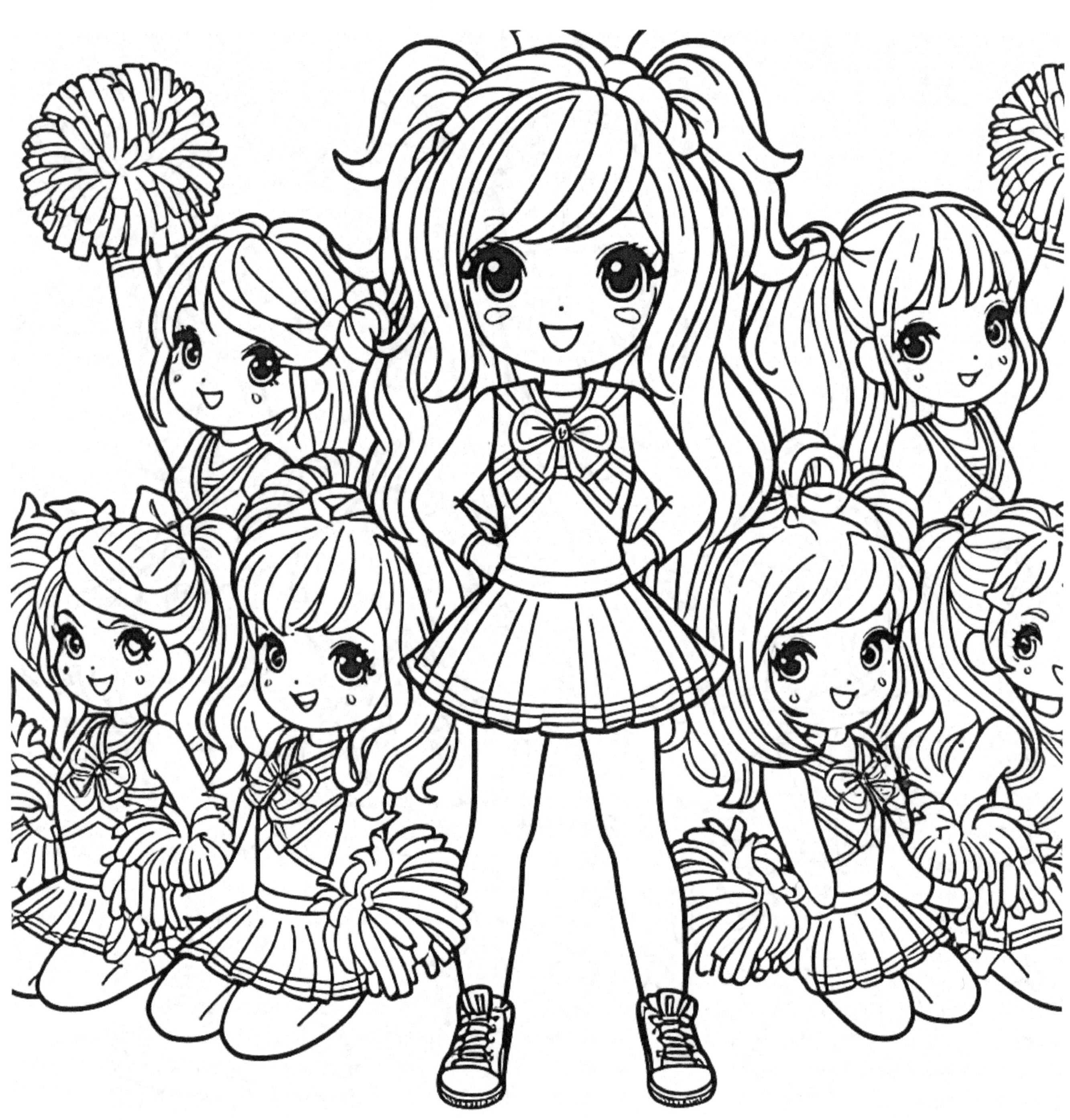